DEDUCT
YOUR HOME

Why a Home Business Offers So
Many Significant, Immediate And Lasting;
Business, Taxation, Wealth And Lifestyle
Benefits

FRANK GENOVESI

DEDUCT YOUR HOME

Why a Home Business Offers So Many Significant,
Immediate and Lasting; Business, Taxation,
Wealth and Lifestyle Benefits

By

FRANK GENOVESI

Fellow of the National Tax & Accountant's Association
Real Estate & Business Sales Professional (WA)
Diploma Financial Services (Financial Planning)
ASIC Registered Agent
Registered Tax Agent
Business Adviser
Proprietor

Website: www.intellisolve.com.au
LinkedIn: https://au.linkedin.com/in/frankgenovesi
Email: frank@intellisolve.com.au
Skype: genovesi111

Published for Genovesi Enterprises Pty Ltd by Evolve Global Publishing
PO Box 327, Stanhope Gardens, NSW, 2768
Email: info@evolveglobalpublishing.com
Website: www.evolveglobalpublishing.com
BookLayout: © 2017 Evolve Global Publishing

ISBN: 978-0-6481966-3-1 (Paperback)
ISBN: 978-0-6481966-1-7 (Hardcover)
ISBN-13: 978-0-6481966-2-4 (Createspace)
ISBN-10: 0648196623   (Createspace)
ISBN: 978-0-6481966-3-1(Smashwords)
ASIN: B076KCDMR8 (Amazon Kindle)

The ATO Acknowledges Our Intellectual Property:

Across a series of rare moves, the Australian Taxation Office has formally admitted our intellectual property both verbally and in writing, as regarding the matter of the taxation of home businesses.

This is significant being that as you may know, a private binding ruling (PBR), is the highest and best form of protection any taxpayer can have as it provides the Commissioner's views in writing to a stated arrangement (or scheme as the ATO calls it), that the taxpayer wants addressed, all for sake of certainty under the tax law. Presuming a PBR is issued, the ATO publishes it at the Register of Private Binding Rulings some 28 days afterward (https://www.ato.gov.au/rba/ search/). This now publicly available document is always edited however to protect the identity of the taxpayer. The register exists to instil community confidence in our tax system by way of a transparent regulator i.e. the ATO (and that's a very good thing in my opinion). I have taken it further however given that in my many interactions with the Australian Taxation Office (ATO), I have put forward both orally and in writing, that much of what I've figured out is the product of my own mind albeit in a format as owned by my company i.e. that it is confidential business information or put interchangeably, intellectual property (IP).

The relevance here is that often times I have obtained private binding rulings for myself, my company and its clients whereby in the process, I have asked the ATO to refrain from putting this IP on public display being it is in the public interest to allow only myself and my company as the developer of the IP, to commercialise it for public consumption. This is important because of the countless reckless advisers who and contrary to the warnings at the register not to do so, would nevertheless read the PBR's at the register and then armed solely with a limited understanding therefrom, would try to reverse engineer them so they could sell to others the advice and outcomes as their own. In my view that would be a recipe for disaster for taxpayers. I therefore take this opportunity to again gratefully acknowledge the ATO's cooperation in each and every instance of having granted my requests. Importantly, all ATO staff must follow published directives from the Commissioner of Taxation known as Law Administration Practice Statements. The relevant one in this case is PSLA 2008/4 where you will see how this process is applied at Step 4: "Remove or replace confidential information"... *https://www.ato. gov.au/law/view/document?docid=PSR/PS20084/NAT/ATO/00001*

Of course, should the so-claimed confidential information already exist in the public domain, then ATO staff must refuse the request. Furthermore, all decisions are reviewed by a higher ranking ATO officer before being handed down to the applicant who requested the PBR.

Interestingly back in 2010, I emailed the Director of Aggressive Tax Planning/Promoter Compliance, Northbridge, WA, to look into my business to ensure it wasn't promoting an illegal tax exploitation scheme under the Promoter Penalty Laws and sure enough she took me up on it. Of course I'm pleased to say here that the letter I received stating that the review had concluded did not indicate any issues and nor have any surfaced since despite it saying the ATO would keep an eye on me. In getting back to the topic of IP, during the second lengthy interview, I directly asked whether or not the IP was mine. The reply given was along the lines of yes the IP is yours but you can't say that we said so. Hmm, even with the acquisition of a few more grey hairs, I'm saying here and now to hell with that silly game as there's no harm in my telling the truth. Of course I still have the cd recording of the "formal review" as was being conducted at the time into all of this and so that is that! The formal review lasted some four months and included perhaps hundreds of emails back and forth plus many telephone calls. I further submitted around 400 pages of technical documents I'd authored and other correspondence including as with the then Federal Treasurer and notable others within government and agencies of government. Of course, none of this means that the ATO has granted myself and/or my company any specific IP rights as that can only be formally done by IP Australia (which on 16/06/2008, granted my company a trade mark for the words "Set Up For Life" (registration number 1245116, as registered on 16/06/2008). "Set Up For Life" is registered in the following classes: Class 35: Business advice; business assistance; business assistance relating to corporate identity; business information; business strategic planning; dissemination of business information; strategic business planning. Class 36: Providing information, including online, about insurance, financial and monetary affairs including real estate affairs;

provision of financial information; provision of information relating to financial services. *https://www.ipaustralia.gov.au/*

In fact, each of the ATO, ASIC and the Tax Practitioners Board have long had a copy of my seminal manuscript entitled "Set Up For Life" i.e. the precursor to this book and which is far more technically orientated towards taxation and other financial professionals.

Table of Contents

Acknowledgement

Let there be no doubt that this book is a game changer across the relevant interrelated fields of business, taxation, property and financial planning and that I researched and wrote it all myself. With this said, I did NOT however "live" through it alone and nor did I solely bear all the risk and associated burdens in having dared challenge the status quo of the various local, state and Federal governments of the day, the Commonwealth agencies that regulate the spaces I operate in, various accounting and financial planning professional associations of the day and a great number of large, intermediate and small firms practising in these areas.

I therefore am indebted to the following good souls for helping me along the journey:

- Michael Carbone, my previous accountant from many years before I got myself into all this and whom helped me realise early on that I was onto something potentially massive and who encouraged me into seriously taking this on this mammoth project.
- Steve Williams (FIPA), for his belief and support throughout.
- John Ardino (CFP), for being such a good listener and having a real go despite not getting to the finish line.
- Chris Wakeford (entrepreneur), for the many conversations about this and that, all of which helped me be the best disrupter I can be in order to do my bit to help people and the planet.
- George Allan (amazing artist and former heady businessman), just for being himself and keeping my radar true.
- Bob Cathcart (retired businessman), for many long lunches where I gleaned bits and pieces of savvy otherwise "not for sale".
- Chester Edwards (pilot and technical writer), for meticulously prufe reeding thsi bookk (sorry my good man but I couldn't resist)!
- And most of all, to my wonderful wife Beatrice for staying the course through thick and thin, especially when obstinance,

arrogance, bitterness, aggressiveness, madness, incompetence, formal tax reviews and lengthy tax audits coupled with ridiculous threats of referrals to other Commonwealth agencies for further investigation as well as threats of litigation by ignorant ATO bullies who operated well behind protected veils yet lacked the requisite substance to see it through. All up, it absolutely wreaked financial ruin upon us being I lost our family home and nearly went bankrupt over this. The humiliation was deep for a financial adviser I can assure you. The industry I had known for more than two decades was almost certainly out-of- bounds to me now. One by one, various people and institutions took their turn upon me and yet nothing they ever did even came close to landing the killer blow they hoped for. Today, the suite of strategies are more amazing and robust than ever and thanks again to my wife for her unbelievable tolerance throughout, here I am today having done nothing wrong and a lot right to be able to offer you this most unique and extraordinary educational material.

Foreword

Intended Audience

> Professionals
> Small Business Owners
> Employees and Families of Those Above
> Anyone Willing To Embark Upon An Enjoyable Journey of Planning
> For and Working Towards A Better Life

Background:

My company currently owns and runs Intellisolve, a professional public business and taxation advice practice as further complimented by real estate, financial information and other services.

Intellisolve's Mission Statement: "To give a sustained boost to your personal and business; financial, retirement, taxation and property affairs".

Fiercely independent, Intellisolve has no bias to any bank, insurer, financial product manufacturer, property developer or anyone else for that matter!

Being focused solely on helping you to accurately identify opportunities, threats and issues across a wide spectrum, Intellisolve empowers you with the requisite blend of knowledge and incentive for you to make timely and astute business and personal decisions and to then get on with helping you to put those decisions into action.

In 1992, I, Gianfranco (Frank) Genovesi (Intellisolve's principal), commenced as a self-employed financial planner to have subsequently helped around one thousand people to build and protect their wealth thus as to achieve or to move much closer to achieving their goals.

In 2005, I gained WA real estate industry sales qualifications also to have worked as both a buyers' and sellers' agent's representative. I have buying and selling residential and commercial property experience in both private treaties and auctions.

From 2001 to the present and via an individually designed and ongoing immersion program, I invested in excess of 14,000 hours of my time in order to now demonstrate a unique expertise across a substantial array of applying the tax law to both personal and small business circumstances (often intertwined and not dissimilar to the sort of commitment as required to complete a bachelor's degree and to follow it up with a masters and then to knock a big dent into a PhD).

This substantial body of experience in navigating a myriad of ATO administrative procedures further expanded to include gaining an outstanding understanding of taxpayer and ATO engagement and behaviour within the Administrative Appeals Tribunal and the courts on matters of objections to taxation assessments and private rulings.

According to some, so broad and so strong is my documented and demonstrated knowledge of how to interpret and apply the tax law, that in November 2012, the Tax Practitioners Board (TPB), approved my application to be a "Registered Tax Agent" (unrestricted), without having prior graduated with a diploma or typically a degree in accountancy, coupled with years of supervised work experience (i.e. the overwhelmingly common pathway to gaining TPB registration). Of note, not even lawyers can achieve this feat without firstly passing a Board approved course in Australian taxation law.

Interestingly, in April 2013 amidst a case I was running, I had somewhat of a run-in with an ATO tax lawyer in front of Senior Member CR Walsh of the Administrative Appeals Tribunal and where the lawyer said to the Tribunal words to the effect I was not an expert in my field. Well that kind of "got up my nose" so I wrote to the TPB to inquire on its position of whether it was ok for me to say that I am such an expert and to have further supplied the Board with some prior blog posts in which I'd blown my own trumpet to that effect. On 06th May 2014, the TPB wrote back to me stating that my conduct in question had NOT breached the tax agent's professional code of conduct (which requires a registered tax agent to act with honesty, integrity and competence and wherein those blogs I effectively stated that):

1. I was Australia's sole trainer to the financial, legal and accounting professions in the above regard and;
2. The ATO had a problem with admitting the fact that I am Australia's foremost expert in my field. (I am further humbled that unlike typical accountants and upon my direct inquiry, the TPB did not require me to complete a Board Approved Course in Australian commercial law to enable the renewal of my tax agent triennial registration. As the gatekeeper to who may become and who may remain a registered tax agent and as a sister Commonwealth agency to the ATO with which it cooperates closely, in conclusion hereof, I take the opportunity to state my gratitude to the Tax Practitioners Board for its continued faith in my technical prowess and associated competence, practices, professionalism and ethics.)

So while I am not degree qualified, I challenge anyone in the world to debate me in any field whatsoever as related to the betterment of home business owners being quite simply, that within my 14,000 hours or so of dedication to mastery in this arena, I never encountered another soul with what could be fairly described as a "good handle" on how it all fits together like a jigsaw puzzle and that includes a substantial number of employees across various government departments and agencies.

My many years in the trenches, battle scars and all, are indeed my badge of honour whereas if that's not good enough for you then my suggestion is for you to open your mind to new possibilities that aren't taught at university etc otherwise, to close this book right now and to do something else with your precious time as if you only care about the formalities but not the realities of life, then clearly we're not compatible.

Frank Genovesi

- Diploma Financial Services (Financial Planning)
- Certificate IV Accounting
- ASIC RG146 SMSF accredited to advise upon and facilitate the establishment and ongoing administration of self-managed superannuation funds.
- Fellow of the National Tax & Accountants' Association Ltd (NTAAF), Membership No. 61871
- NTAA Public Accountant Member of the (NTAA+), as Stapled to NTAA Membership No. 61871.
- ASIC Registered Agent No. 34341 (via Genovesi Enterprises Pty Ltd)
- WA Registered Real Estate and Business Sales Representative No. 51176 (holder of Diploma of Property Services [Agency Management])
- Small business owner/operator since 1993

Various Capacities To Act:

Property: I provide advice and services in relation to any requirement to hold, develop, sell or buy your home, your home business property, your residential or commercial investment property and/or your business real property.

Taxation & Accounting Services: You may instruct Intellisolve to collect, classify and interpret your financial information and as registered tax agents, to further serve you with associated taxation compliance and/or advisory functions.

As a registered tax agent, Intellisolve can:

- Register you or your entity for GST
- Obtain a tax file number for you or your entity
- Advise upon the most suitable business structure
- Preparation and lodgement of your personal and business, company, trust and SMSF tax returns
- Preparation and lodgement of BAS and PAYG Withholding

º   Representing your dealings with the Commissioner of Taxation as may be required from time to time by way of applications and objections on a range of matters such as assessments, private and class rulings, audit findings, Administrative Appeals Tribunal matters etc.).

Small Business Services: Intellisolve can register your small business for an ABN, assist with dealings with local councils to obtain development approvals to commence or vary a business and more. Furthermore as an ASIC Registered Agent, Intellisolve can also serve as your company's registered office for purposes of liaison with ASIC, setting up companies and special purpose companies and more. (Note): All general insurance, legal, leasing and loan finance matters are outsourced upon your consent to trusted associates.

Perspective:

It may surprise you that in my holding multiple qualifications and running a professional practice that serves every day employed and self-employed clients, that over the last 10 or more years, whenever I have attended industry professional development days and other relevant professional educational events, that I've always been both shocked and relieved to find that no professional firms, associations, bodies or speakers of any persuasion, have ever even attempted to explain to the room full of practitioners like myself, just how anything like this can help them to meet their clients' needs and moreover, that it even exists.

In fact, in the 25 years of my financial planning career, I've never met anyone who has claimed to have "created" any type of financial product or strategy as worth discussing let alone going to the trouble of writing a book about it.

From time to time in various Parliaments, a politician holds an opposing personal conviction of conscience and yet is bound to abide by a strict party room rule whereby he or she is prohibited from crossing the floor to vote with the other side because the government lacks the numbers to otherwise survive a vote on a bill. Similarly, I know that tens of thousands of accountants and financial planners in public practice are all pretty much ignorant of what I have worked out and worse still, they lack the fortitude to stand against the status quo that is largely driven by the banks, fund managers, insurance companies, professional indemnity insurers, professional associations and regulators. To put it mildly, I think it's disgraceful!

By comparison, I happily make up my own rules within "the rules" as that's the exact mindset needed to come up with anything even remotely legal but sexy when you operate within the rigid confines of financial services and taxation.

Specifically in terms of home businesses, what I will unveil soon is refreshingly clear, simple and beautiful as it all plays with your heart more than with the head (or so it seems until a closer look will reveal to you how it's very much equally driven by the numbers).

Also and for what it's worth, I'm pretty casual as I can't remember the last time I wore a tie for work (it's usually jeans and an open-neck shirt or even a tee shirt). I often spend my days at home in front of a laptop doing my thing in between running around like a headless chook as I try to fit in with my three kids' hectic schedules plus getting dinner ready (my wife works full-time). Oh and I typically rehearse with and play in two or three rock bands at a time (which also sees me running around here and there day and night - but hey I love it or I wouldn't be doing it)! I also have my fingers in other business pies and am happy to look at other things from time to time if and when I have a moment. What I'm really saying here is that my flexible work-life balance means a lot to me as it allows me to pretty much do it all on my terms and this is a carry-over of what I've learned and greatly appreciate about home businesses.

At time of writing (Aug 2019, I'm 56 years old) but from around age 27 to 30, I was a heavily gigging musician in and around New York City and up the east coast of the USA. Then upon coming home and where I tried being "normal again", I somehow fell into financial planning where over the next decade, I built a thriving practice in Perth, WA and then Fremantle, WA. I then sold that business with its several hundreds of happy clients so I could semi-retire, never expecting to return to the industry. You see after all that, I was desperate to be a muso again as I felt I'd sold out of my dream just to make money in the big bad world of finance and that the clock was ticking big time or in other words, I was having myself a well-deserved mid-life crisis approaching the big 4... 0!

Next, I sold everything and where for nearly the next two years, I lived a simple life on a small farm that bordered a quaint village, a short drive from Paris, France in which I pursued my then life's dream in recording 55 of 200+ of my own songs and I short-listed these into two full length CD albums. I could barely put a simple sentence together in French when I got there and this was all part of my grand plan to plant myself somewhere that I couldn't be tempted to pursue a decent job or to run a half-intelligent business (as when you're the immigrant who doesn't speak the local language you quickly learn that washing dishes out the back of a restaurant is about where society places you on its socioeconomic totem pole). So yes, I was exactly where I wanted to be as I knew darn well that I'd otherwise succumb to the temptation of chasing the almighty dollar again.

The good news is that my wife worked full time (she's French so that was handy). This allowed me to devote myself to my music again by way of getting my own original band together and in doing heaps of live shows, getting some radio airplay and live radio interviews and even landing a live tv performance on France 3 as the guest artist. I had my album featured in the biggest record store in my home town of Orleans right next to the likes of Sting and Bruce Springsteen etc (hey I was considered an international artist) and I felt pretty good about it all as I was definitely getting there but due to family matters and other pressures, I had to pull the pin and come home.

I'd also like to add that even though it was a great time of my life and that I do miss it sometimes, I've definitely moved on from wanting to be a rock-star and that the relevance of my telling you about my musical life to your wanting to know why having a home business is such a cool idea is two-fold:

1. If I hadn't have gone to France, the IP simply would not exist as it was there that it began to germinate whilst recording my albums (must've been something in the clean farm and surrounding forest air) and;
2. Nowadays, I'm quite happy to run a little home business that brings me in a few bucks but where I get to come home to my family at nights as opposed to my touring days and this is simply me gigging around the local Perth scene and having myself a mighty good time in the process and that if I can turn a hobby into a business, if need be, then maybe you can too!

Back to point one above, there's got to be something said for huge amounts of open space, fresh air and peace and quiet because believe me that life on the farm was generally very bloody quiet (except of course for when I was recording scorching guitar solos or live drum tracks that you would've heard in the forest behind the farm). Oh yes, the forest ... around 30,000 hectares of wild oak forest was my daily backdrop beyond the fields. The long walks immersed within a stunning array of flora and fauna was breathtaking and it liberated me from the years I had spent in front of a computer going over client portfolios etc.

I would sometimes contemplate my old life in Australia and think how all the people I knew in the "game" were running around like busy bees trying to get the next client, the next fee, the next commission, the next deal etc and not get hauled over the coals for something or even be sued in the process, What a rat race I thought and I was just so happy to be out of it.

I also realised that none of them had any spare time or head space to be able to even step back a little let alone drop out like I had. Effectively I came to the indisputable conclusion that they had no hope at all of finding new and better ways of playing the game while they were still neck deep in it.

There's an old and very true saying that you need to sometimes work on your business rather than in it whereas I took it to a combined whole of industries approach.

This awesome, peaceful environment that was so far removed from my old life gave me the opportunity to "change on the inside" as in between writing and recording songs and rehearsing for live shows with my original band, I was subconsciously drafting ideas that were related to my prior life as a financial planner but my fresh perspective was derived from living a new life on my own terms.

Within a few months of returning home to Australia, I was possessed.

I stayed up all hours writing down the ideas I had formulated in France. One after another they poured and poured. It was unstoppable and it was beautiful.

I was scared, excited and bewildered but at the same time very calm and purposeful in my ways of being.

I could barely think of anything else for a very long time ... that's right ... about the next six years, hence the 14,000 (ish) hours.

So and from the time before I left France and through to my first year of having returned home, this huge surprise "penny" which had dropped from the sky and to have landed squarely upon me, had morphed into a realisation that I'd stumbled across a new way of going about financial planning and business planning and that tax was just a piece of the puzzle, albeit one of the key drivers.

Going to France was part of a "two year plan" that included legally not having to pay any capital gains tax (CGT), on the proceeds of the financial planning business I'd sold. Therefore and to ensure that outcome in accordance with an Australian Taxation Office (ATO) Private and Binding Ruling (PBR), that I'd received prior to departure from the Federal Commissioner of Taxation (the Commissioner), I returned home within two years of selling the business and I re-entered Australia intent on continuing as a professional singer/songwriter/musician.

It's funny how things don't always go to plan as that profound "penny" which dropped in France was set to overtake me and become my main new business, not music (sob, sob).

I'm an optimist but not a blind one as I also knew that the financial planning industry and taxation profession had never considered anything like this before and that the going would be very tough in trying to convince the status quo that I was "onto something" but damn I was up for it!

Context Is Key:

What have I got myself into I thought as I quickly found myself up to my ears and then over my head. By necessity, I evolved into something akin to an endurance athlete as I was at times un-knotting whilst at others piecing together, entire bodies of legislation and/or sub-sections thereof in regards to; Australian Commonwealth Corporations Law, several Commonwealth Acts on taxation law, superannuation law, financial services law and a heap of common law as well as many state-based legislative acts.

Furthermore, I was delving into a plethora of centuries-old long-established legal doctrines and professional practices and ethics (not all of which were flattering upon any diligent observation or analysis).

All the while I was deciphering, clarifying and giving meaning where little or none appeared to exist, to what I determined were the newly and necessarily required legal and practical cross-considerations and applications in the fields of:

- Federal, state and local authority taxation
- Real estate and conveyance (i.e. in terms of the buying, selling and holding of property and privately owned small businesses)
- Finance
- Accounting
- Financial planning

Such things when considered in the unique context I'd put forward, had become inextricably embroiled to an incredibly intense level as never previously anticipated by anyone including myself. As it was, no one person seemed sufficiently professionally qualified nor held any significant body of direct and/or related experience such that they could undoubtedly confirm the legality and overall soundness nor appropriateness of what appeared to have been accomplished.

It therefore became a matter of my piecing together various segments of information and then making them fit into one big picture that now comprises my company's Strategies or "schemes" as the ATO likes to call them (bearing in mind that not all "schemes" are bad)!

My company has claimed the fruit of this monumental "dot-connecting" project it as its "Intellectual Property" (IP). That is not to say however, that the hundreds of individual truths that have long existed in the public domain and which are encapsulated in this work are my company's IP as that would be ridiculous. In this respect, I refer to things like financial planning, legal, taxation and real estate concepts and applicable laws etc. I simply wish to reiterate that after what has transpired since around 2001 when this all started, that I've put it all on the line i.e. considerable personal determination, sacrifice, toil and money and along with the significant associated opportunity cost, all as expended in conducting my research and in testing it out on myself and others. To date, I estimate a personal cost of around $4,000,000 that can be attributed to the creation and development of the IP.

Clearly the IP has no competition as I've yet to find any other body of work that even begins to tie it all together such that the various conclusions that have been drawn within, have been fastidiously and clearly established from Statutory and other Proper Authority wherever possible and at all times with due skill and care. Furthermore the IP stands alone as the only type in existence to have been tested by Australia's regulators (and successfully)!

Upon returning to Perth and after a short while, I embarked on a new career as a buyer's agent for a very prominent Subiaco based real estate buying and valuation firm. Principally, I believe I was hired for the qualities they appreciated given my extensive knowledge and successful background as a financial planner. They knew the analytical and communication skills I'd developed would make the going relatively easy for me as I was keen to provide "advisory" services in real estate rather than just flogging houses for the most I could get being as that's what sellers generally expect. Whilst a buyers agency is run so much more like a financial planning practise than a selling agency due to having to substantiate a recommendation to buy a property via a comprehensive report as based upon the client's situation and requirements, nonetheless, I quickly and unfortunately realised that it was seriously lagging behind financial planning in terms of overall compliance, attention to a great many details and other matters.

No matter I thought as during this tenure I tried in vain to convince many local financial planners to collaborate with me to ensure clients' would obtain qualified and licensed financial advice hand in hand with the property advice I could now provide but unfortunately nobody was interested in playing ball or more to the point, that for their own sakes, everyone was seemingly guarding their clients against any influence from other advisers or so it unfortunately appeared.

Several months passed and I'd had enough so I switched back into financial planning joining a WA based, national firm as an Authorised Representative of this Australian Financial Services Licensee (AFSL). Again I busted my backside in pushing established boundaries by contacting many local real estate agents to hopefully create alliances for the benefit of clients but was met with even more apathy than ever before. I could barely get any agents to return my calls to discuss my ideas. In desperation, I placed an advertisement in my local community newspaper (and one that was a bastion for local real estate advertising), inviting highly ethical real estate agents to contact me for details on how I as a financial planner could help their clients and themselves to prosper but you guessed it, noone responded!

After about 18 months of continuing to toil and getting nowhere, I made the decision to abandon both the real estate and financial planning industries as an adviser/representative to instead devote myself to refining and commercialising the IP. As I went along, I met with the WA state managers of two national real estate sales franchises who thought I was mad to even try to get the property and financial advice industries to work together to help clients (now what does that tell you)? I also approached many of the largest bank and non-bank owned financial planning businesses in Australia in the hope they would see the light but I failed to get any traction beyond one or two meetings being their concerns typically amounted to either or all of:

1. A denial that I'd figured out anything of substance to which their technical teams were unaware.
2. A deep fear of any potential for "brand damage" should firstly the ATO catch-wind and then the media and;
3. An instinctive reluctance to promote customers pursuing direct real estate purchases or building extensions (including even their own homes), rather than the artificial, manufactured financial investment products that their advisers could "distribute" for them.

Preface To The Strategies

These are an intertwined assortment of business, wealth and lifestyle "Strategies" with consequential, inseparable tax benefits and not the other way around.

So it is with the utmost of absolute good faith that I commend this book to you in the hope you'll make a better life for yourself, whatever that may be.

FRANK GENOVESI

Fellow of the National Tax & Accountant's Association
Real Estate & Business Sales Professional (WA)
Diploma Financial Services (Financial Planning)
ASIC Registered Agent
Registered Tax Agent
Business Adviser
Proprietor

Frank Genovesi

1 - So What's All The Fuss About?

In short, there are four reasons to be excited and to keep reading:

1. You're about to become very well informed about a "platform" that enables you to experience the least expensive way ever known to own and run any Australian business as legally capable of being run at or from your current and/or future home.
2. This same platform enables you to enjoy the least expensive way ever known to own and run your home regardless of what it is, where it is, how much it's worth and whether or not it's currently owned, mortgaged or rented.
3. You can then either spend, save or invest the resulting savings (or any combination thereof), at your whim and this can be done privately and/or through or your business and;
4. You can vastly improve the standard of your home and thus your lifestyle, all at the lowest possible cost.

A well-planned and executed home business strategy simultaneously enriches your personal and business wealth and your lifestyle, via unique, advanced, unrivalled and vastly superior, property, financial planning and taxation analysis and strategic optimisation.

Many of the following benefits can result:

º Keeps you in full control of your business, lifestyle and investment agenda and decisions
º Allows you the opportunity even if you're not well off
º Lowers the cost of home ownership at any purchase price
º Upgrades you into a better home in a better suburb at less net cost than any other way
º Adds extra space to your current loved home at less net cost than any other way
º Allows you to take advantage even if you're renting

- Allows you to convert your job into a business for extra clout
- Saves on Doubled-Up Commercial Property Expenses
- Allows you to benefit even if you've already paid off your home
- Allows you to invest any cost savings
- Allows you to invest any tax savings.
- Allows you to put any savings against your home loan
- Allows capital growth on your superior home business property to work for you
- Allows you to renovate or extend i.e. add value for less
- Allows you to take the opportunity to create equity as soon as you upgrade your home
- Allows you to enjoy and/or invest any capital gains tax upon future sale of your home business property that would otherwise be payable
- Wipes out your mortgage faster
- Wipes out or greatly reduces your consolidated non tax-deductible personal debts e.g. personal loans and credit cards
- Provides you with an average six figure, tax free windfall
- Easily beats the First Home Owners Grant by letting you or someone you love into a property so you both win financially for years to come
- Allows you to claim a wide range of business tax deductions on your existing and unavoidable expenses as connected to your main residence (i.e. mortgage interest, building insurance, council rates, repairs and maintenance and utilities)
- Allows you to claim building depreciation
- Positions yourself for very little and very possibly even no capital gains tax payable upon any future sale of your home
- Allows you to have less tax taken out of your regular pay from your usual job
- Allows you to run your home business either full-time or "on-the-side"
- Allows you to choose whatever type of business you like (providing it complies locally)
- Allows you to change businesses at your discretion
- Helps the environment
- Allows for tax effective travel

º   Allows for tax effective motoring
º   Allows for tax effective home furnishings
º   Allows for tax effective non-tax deductible areas of your home such as gourmet kitchens, alfresco and swimming pools (and that's not a typo)
º   Either boosts or annihilates your superannuation as a retirement vehicle
º   Creates future opportunities to leverage into other investments
º   Enriches your lifestyle now and forever in ways that apparently no one else has ever before dreamed as being possible
º   Caters to your own age, level of wealth and business, employment and personal circumstances in harnessing the powerful effects of treating part of your home as a place of business
º   Safely and surely helps you by virtue of having been in constant development since 2002 via many detailed engagements with the ATO and particularly in having obtained many PBR's from the ATO

Please accept that none of us can have everything on the above list being we all have unique current and future circumstances that determine what direction or directions this will take and just how far one can go with it. Effectively therefore, the following are all potential factors that will influence the outcomes for you:

º   Your current and/or proposed business structure
º   The number of and type/s of businesses you already do or will operate
º   The type and size of your home property
º   The size of your family
º   Quality of relationships with partners and children
º   Your debts and obligations
º   Your ability to borrow money
º   Your available cash or other reasonably liquid assets
º   Your work ethic
º   Your tolerance for an adjusted work/home life
º   Your income or lack thereof from other jobs
º   Your income or lack thereof from other businesses
º   Your success or otherwise in being "in business"

- º Your general intelligence Your business and investment savvy
- º And more!

To date, I've identified thirty-eight settled everyday scenarios regarding ownership structure and operation of any one or more **genuine home businesses of your choice**. Having identified a widespread failure in the thinking of the taxation profession, generally speaking, you can now stop losing a lot of money as the IP allows you to claim running expenses (i.e. extra heating, lighting and phone etc) and more importantly occupancy expenses (i.e. mortgage interest or rent, building insurance plus council and water rates), far beyond the norm and all without necessarily having to pay any CGT upon potential future profitable sale of your home.

Furthermore, you can often claim thousands of dollars extra per annum in notional building depreciation expenses i.e. without paying any money out to get the deduction except for ordering a once-off building taxation depreciation schedule.

I condemn anyone or any firm or other entity who might seek to benefit from my company's IP without running a real home business and the same goes for any practitioner who advises clients to create a sham business to try and cheat against the vast majority of taxpayers who do the right thing.

When selling an investment or business for example, it's good that if you dig around you can almost always find a tax adviser who will likely furnish what can only be described as highly effective mainstream tax advice and where if he or she is really good, they'll ensure the advice is tempered with equally excellent financial planning advice, legal advice and related implementation. It would likely be hard to find an unhappy client or adviser when the end result is a non-taxable major transaction given that seems to be the "end game" i.e. in seeking out the advice.

From where I sit however, that's plainly insufficient as I strive to use a low or no tax event as a starting point from which to create a broader optimum scenario of additional tax-effective wealth creation that goes hand-in-hand with lifestyle enhancement as beyond the imagination of other advice firms.

The IP can reside within an existing home business, within many and varied existing non-home businesses or within a new home business venture and across varying ownership structures, irrespective if the intended user has other full or part time business or employment commitments.

Implementing the IP in accordance with the ATO's non-commercial loss rules, high income earning PAYG taxpayers can offset up to $250,000 p.a. (or $500,000 per coupled household), of such otherwise taxable "other" income in any given financial year. If you're an average income earner though with modest mortgage, you can typically look at claiming in the range of $20,000 – $50,000 p.a in new deductions.

There is no small business deduction limit upon private companies that employ the IP.

In concert with meeting the basic conditions to enable invocation of the small business CGT concessions, you'll need to ensure you meet the ATO definition of a small business as and when appropriate, the main ones being that annual turnover must be under $2M and for net tangible business assets to be under $6M. This is sufficient to capture the vast majority of people who would consider doing this. E.g. a $10M mansion with a $5M mortgage on it from within which a business turns over $1.999M p.a qualifies (generally speaking).

2 - Resimercial (Our Infused, Asset Sub - Class)

The four main asset classes are:

1. Property
2. Shares
3. Fixed Interest
4. Cash

Each of the above have many sub-classes.

As property is the subject of the day, we'll now break down its major subclasses:

1. Industrial
2. Commercial
3. Rural and;
4. Residential

Given we're concentrating on the astute exploitation of a main residence (as a part-business asset), the following is a reasonably comprehensive break down of the residential sub-class:

- Vacant Land
- Houses
- Terrace Houses
- Duplexes
- Triplexes
- Quadruplexes
- Larger Grouped Dwellings
- Townhouses
- Villas

- ᵒ Units
- ᵒ Flats/Apartments
- ᵒ Condominiums
- ᵒ Penthouses
- ᵒ Lofts
- ᵒ Warehouse Conversions
- ᵒ Permanent Park Homes
- ᵒ Caravans & Houseboats (what the heck ... we're on a roll)!

I'm sure there are more but this will do for the moment.

Whilst these buildings are usually found in residential areas, there are many exceptions such as mixed use zones (inner CBD, redeveloped commercial or residential zones etc). Of note, in such areas, you'll also find houses that have been converted to professional suites etc with the substantive point however, being that residential buildings are mainly used for residential purposes.

When you decide to start a small business, you have a number of options in terms of how it is to operate and from where it is to be based. E.g. in a:

- ᵒ Home
- ᵒ Office
- ᵒ Studio
- ᵒ Mobile Business
- ᵒ On-Site (e.g. professional contractor, trades-person, performing artist etc)
- ᵒ Factory / Workshop
- ᵒ Hobby farm/market garden, horticulture, viticulture etc

Whilst there may be others, I'm certainly struggling to think of any at the moment!

Looking at this list, only four (home, on-site, mobile, rural etc), are sufficiently flexible for these purposes because they can each be carried on within a home as being the principal "place of business".

On the contrary, if you have say a separate office, studio or workshop etc and you take your work home either occasionally or regularly, the ATO does NOT allow you to claim occupancy expense deductions for areas within your home where you do the work. The Commissioner's view was clearly established on 30/09/1993 in taxation ruling TR 93/30 and subsequently upheld by the courts, that such an area or areas will be merely considered a "home study" and this is true even if that is the ONLY activity conducted in that part of the home.

Confused?

Think about it…

You're generally not allowed to live in an office, studio, factory or workshop etc, right? Also you can't claim your home mortgage and other occupancy expenses because the generally accepted wisdom amongst accountants is that it isn't worth the dreaded CGT implications and so if you been listening to these types, you've likely missed out on claiming thousands every year in normal business deductions on your home.

I'm saying **there's nothing better than incurring a whopping-big-fat CGT liability** when you sell your home and this is because firstly you must have:

- ⚬ Made money at sale
- ⚬ Been smart enough throughout to ensure your business passed an ATO test called the **"interest deductibility test"**
- ⚬ **Again been smart enough to have exercised your entitlement** to claim a good part of if not all of the mortgage interest plus a good part of water and council rates, building insurance and building depreciation expenses (and more) and all for many years as you enjoyed the ride leading up to your BIG PAY DAY!

And so here it is … "RESIMERCIAL"

"INFUSED", RESIDENTIAL / COMMERCIAL PROPERTY

And here's what **"Resimercial Property"**, i.e. what we're declaring as the word's latest asset sub-class currently looks and feels like:

Sure, it looks and feels like residential property but check out these key features:

- Zoned residential
- Comes in any floor plan (multi-level/guest wings/open-plan/ rooms off a long corridor/ alfresco areas/ bits of everything – it doesn't matter)
- Can be GST free at sale (unlike commercial property), albeit where GST must apply at sale, the GST margin scheme can be applied.
- A wide range of home business & or home occupations are allowed to operate within by practically all Australian local governments
- Contrary what appears to be widespread among local council in their planning policies, most have no restriction on the amount of floor space that may be allocated for business use
- All bona-fide, typical business property tax deductions can already be claimed under existing legislation (e.g. same as non, home-based business properties)
- No necessarily practical detrimental effect on CGT main residence exemption per the non-business use of the property (for sole

proprietors, partnerships and private companies) as any CGT raised from business use of the property may be reduced if not totally eliminated using the small business CGT concessions

º Favourably rated by State and Local Governments as residential property (and with certain residential exemptions still applying e.g. land tax)

I'd like to talk turkey with anyone who can explain to me what other asset class or sub-class offers all this upside without any discernible downside.

So there it is – something brand new for you to invest in (and you might already even have one without having to invest anything – just a few tweaks needed here and there I suspect).

3 - Some Pertinent Facts And Worthy Thoughts

1. Australia has around nine million dwellings and around one million people currently working in home businesses.
2. The Australian Government Department of Innovation, Industry, Science and Research published that the home business sector is Australia's largest and fastest growing of all business sectors and that some 96% of all businesses are small business and that 70% of all small businesses are home businesses. Accordingly, 67% of all businesses are home-based with common examples being mobile professionals and tradies.
3. The information technology revolution and the trend away from centralisation of employees will only see the market grow.
4. Mortgage interest and taxation and are most people's largest expense.
5. Personal and corporate insolvencies and bankruptcies are through the roof.
6. Banks are experiencing record profits.
7. The ATO is ever more aggressive and sophisticated at detecting taxpayer avoidance and evasion.
8. The IP serves as a powerful disincentive to participate in the cash economy as you can usually be financially better off in following the law, thereby eliminating risk of prosecution.
9. Many people are hurting financially and crying out for relief.
10. Many people have still not recovered from the global financial crisis.
11. Many people want empathy with their life situation, not just clever financial and/or taxation advice.
12. Many people want to live better NOW as well as be better off in the future however no one really knows how to help as growth investments such as shares and property are dangerous for short-term dabbling and safety-conscious fixed-income based investments require extremely large sums to be invested in order

to return anything noteworthy and particularly during what is a current and likely continuing record low-interest rate global environment not to forget there is really no way to reap any lifestyle enhancement from these along the way.

13. Many people have an inherent misunderstanding and mistrust of financial advisers.

14. Many people equally don't particularly like or trust lawyers and realtors but are forced to use them mainly due to being too lazy or time poor to do the required work to educate themselves as to what is required in their situation.

15. Most practicing public accountants are so time and resource poor they lack the energy or inclination to pursue the creation and provision of IP as comparable to this. Furthermore, the prohibitive development costs would be unbearable if imposed upon clients in order to reap even a modest commercially viable return on investment. Finally, an undertaking of this magnitude would require taking their eyes off the ball for so long that their core business would suffer badly.

16. It's a fresh "platform" upon which you can run a business, create long term wealth through property and by other means and simultaneously enrich your lifestyle as you go.

17. It combines a significant and potent array of features and benefits as otherwise unavailable from each of government, realtors, lawyers, financial planners and accountants.

18. This "stuff" isn't taught anywhere else.

19. Back in 2009, I brought my business operation and aims to the written attention of the then Federal Treasurer The Hon Wayne Swan MP and the then Commissioner of Taxation Mr Michael D'Ascenzio. I asked the Treasurer to discuss my ideas with the Commissioner and to revert thereafter with any joint qualms or issues etc. The response I received was on the letterhead of The Office of The Federal Treasurer, Canberra and it included to the effect that discussions had occurred with the Commissioner as regards to my home business proposals as put to the government and that The Commissioner said that if I wanted my clients to have certainty under the law, that they should apply for an ATO private binding ruling (PBR), on how my company's home business proposals would affect them.

20. A materially positive PBR effectively gives you the government's formal protection to proceed with this IP with more certainty than is otherwise possible any other way under our country's current political, Australian Public Service and legislative environment.
21. PBR's are issued free of charge by the ATO.
22. I next set about creating highly advanced templates encompassing the IP for this specific purpose.
23. Unless mismanaged, the IP provides a far more accumulative tax effective investment environment than superannuation and that includes each of public, industry, retail or self-managed superannuation funds (SMSF), being there are no earnings or contribution taxes. There are also no annual audit requirements. It also dovetails beautifully with superannuation for tax-free pension phase benefits (please consider here the potential application of the CGT small business retirement concession). Additionally, it allows generous use of business assets within business use areas of a family home (e.g. art, antiques etc), that would not survive the application of the Superannuation Industry Supervision Act in respect of SMSF's. Furthermore, there are no early access issues being that "preservation" until a "condition of release" is not a consideration. There is an undeniably high risk of receiving severe punitive treatment from the ATO to trustees of a SMSF should their ongoing observance of all the rules and regulations not be of a very high standard.
24. You will most likely qualify to do this (mainly subject though to your work-life attitude).
25. You could possibly soon upgrade into any new or established home of your choice, with no location restrictions and for less net cost than any other way.
26. Alternatively to (25) above, you can stay in your current home to still benefit by immediately wiping-out or seriously reducing your consolidated non-tax-deductible personal debts (e.g; home mortgage, personal loans, credit cards etc).
27. Further to (26) above, if you have low or no home loan debt, the IP can put an average $100,000 windfall into your pocket (based on the average Australian home mortgage of around $350,000 and an average 30% tax rate payable).

28. David Koch is one of Australia's foremost business and finance commentators and is considered one of the 10 most influential people of all time in the financial services industry. The widely known and respected "KOCHIE" as he's affectionately called, also understands just how important the things we talk about are to small business. At the "Kochie's Business Builder" website (www.kochiesbusinessbuilders.com.au), he even put up his own Tax Wish List for Christmas 2009 called "For Christmas I Want...A Simplified Tax System". He went on to say "I thought it might be interesting to put forward a wish list of initiatives". He then said at point (4) (emphasis added) ... "Allow small business owners to claim part of their mortgage payments as a tax deduction when the business is run from home without sacrificing the CGT benefit. At the moment if you claim mortgage repayments as a business deduction you waive your CGT exemption rights on your home. A reversal of this law would really help small business owners". Consequently all I'm saying here is that the misconstrued and limited scope of the potential application of our tax laws in this area clearly extends beyond the tax profession and into other realms such as financial services and expert media commentary. No worries though Kochie as you meant well and you're still a bloody legend!

29. Unlike managed investments, you keep full day-to-day control of your personal and business assets and affairs!

4 - The Five Strategies

In developing what is a unique range, I couldn't resist in giving them cute or dorky names (I'll leave that determination up to you)!

1. **The Small Business Re-Birth (SBRB)**
2. **The Home Business Re-Structure (HBRS)**
3. **The Twist-Exist Re-Structure (TERS)**
4. **The Small Business Lease Buster (SBLB)**
5. **The Co-Owners Wealth Builder (COWB)**

But wait - there's more - because each of them have four (4) subsets as you will see shortly.

With five strategies x four subsets, we have 20 possibilities but to spice things up even more, each of these can be run as either sole traders or partnerships (let's call that Group 1). These can also be run under a company or by a corporate trustee of a family trust (i.e. Group 2).

20 x Group 1 plus 20 x Group 2 makes 40 possibilities except for the fact that due to no replacement active asset being acquired, there can be no Group 1 SBRB (ii) and (iii) in the usual context and whilst the others will retain their usual Roman numeral ID i.e. (i) & (iv). This mumbo jumbo will all hopefully make sense soon.

Therefore you have 38 different structures to consider for your home business and as you become familiar with these, it should become apparent to you which applies to your situation.

Of course I couldn't just leave it at because these can be combined in a number of ways that I call "combos".

Small Business Re-Birth (i)
Sell An Active Business Asset/s & Initially Buy A Home To Live In & From Which To Start a Business.

(e.g. for those renting or living with family).

Small Business Re-Birth (ii)
Sell An Active Business Asset/s & Stay In Current Purchased Home & Start a Business From There.

Small Business Re-Birth (iii)
Sell An Active Business Asset/s & Stay In Current Purchased Home, Extend It & Start a Business From There.

Small Business Re-Birth (iv)
Sell An Active Business Assets/ & Upgrade Your Existing Purchased Home To A Better Home/Better Area - To Live In & From Where To Start a Business.

Home Business Re-Structure (i)
Initially, Buy A Home To Live In & From Where to Start a Business (e.g. for those renting or living with family).

Home Business Re-Structure (ii)
Stay In Current Purchased Home & Start a Business From There.

Home Business Re-Structure (iii)
Stay In Current Purchased Home, Extend It & Start a Business From There.

Home Business Re-Structure (iv)
An Existing Purchaser's Upgrade To A Better Home/Better Area From Where To Live & Start a Business.

Twist Exist Re-Structure (i)
Stop Renting Your Home Business Property, Buy One Instead And Keep Running The Business.

Twist Exist Re-Structure (ii)
Stay In Current Purchased Home & Continue Running Your Existing Home-Based Business.

Twist Exist Re-Structure (iii)
Stay In Current Purchased Home, Extend It, & Continue Running Your Existing Home-Based Business.

Twist Exist Re-Structure (iv)
Upgrade To A Better Home/Better Area & Continue To Run Your Existing Home-Based Business.

Small Business Lease Buster (i)
Initially, Buy A Home To Live In & From Where To Start a Business (e.g.; for those renting or living with family).

Small Business Lease Buster (ii)
Stay In Current Purchased Home & Start a Business From There.

Small Business Lease-Buster (iii)
Stay In Current Purchased Home, Extend It, & Start a Business From There.

Small Business Lease Buster (iv)
An Existing Purchaser's Upgrade To A Better Home/Better Area To Live In & From Where To Start a Business.

Co-Owners Wealth Builder (i)
Initially, Buy A Home To Live In & To Start a Business From.
(E.g. for those renting or living with family or friends).

Co-Owners Wealth Builder (ii)
Extend One Party's Home For All To Comfortably Live In &   To Start a Business From.

Co-Owners Wealth Builder (iii)
Upgrade One Party's Home For All To Live In & From Where To Start a Business.

1. As can be seen and in short, either you're a homeowner or you're not.
2. Subsequently, either you have an existing home based business or you don't.
3. Furthermore, you may or may not have another business or a job.
4. Furthermore, again, you may or may not have an active business asset you no longer want or need.
5. Yet again, if you have a business outside of your home, it may or may not be run from leased premises.
6. At yet another level, close friends, siblings, parents and their children etc may wish to do business together and to own property together where one or more live in the subject property.

In taking expert guidance to select and implement the right strategy, you can take a safe, staged approach to achieving a pre-selected general outcome due to the necessary skill and accuracy having been applied to integrate the IP into the following arenas:

- Financial Planning
- Taxation Planning and Compliance
- Accounting
- Property - Selection, Retention, Development, Improvement, Maintenance and Sales
- Business – Planning, Creation, Mentoring, Sales, Restructuring & Redevelopment
- Legal Solutions
- Mortgage Finance
- Local Council – Required Guidance per the Application & Approvals Process

We have also developed software to determine the right strategy from the extensive menu.

This is not the space for random acts, guess-work or crossing your fingers as when it comes to your money and your personal and business life, it must all make sense, be realistic and be lawful. The IP is a robust set of specialist coordination and guidance principles and instructions, purpose engineered to achieve the safest, highest and most expedited results that anyone has ever dared dream possible and it has subsequently been brought to fruition through my approximate 14,000 hours of detailed research, development and testing in the arenas of government, agency of government and various taxpayers who have put the IP through its paces and to have come out the other end smiling.

Frank Genovesi

5 - If This Is So Good, Why Hasn't My Accountant, Financial Planner Or Lawyer Told Me About It?

Darn that's a good question and it takes a bit of answering!

As prior alluded to, there are no educational institutions in the land that offer a single course even remotely capable of imparting the requisite knowledge as significant units of study across each of taxation and accounting are required to be mixed in with the same in financial planning, property, law, finance, business, general insurance and more.

Also as touched upon, most accountants in public practise are simply far too busy to find a spare few dozen hours let alone a few hundred hours or more to even begin to figure this stuff out (please remember that I have personally invested in excess of 14,000 hours in the trenches to get my unique education of which equates to about 6 years of full-time study).

Through my own means including direct engagement, I know that none of Australia's professional bodies whether they represent accountants, tax agents, financial planners, real estate agents, lawyers or anyone else for that matter, fathom either the depth, the breadth and the subtleties of what is required for their members to competently advise their clients on this specialist intertwined field. This is because the IP comprises a labyrinth of federal and state law, local council policy and guidelines, business advice at all stages of the business lifecycle, taxation, property, wealth creation, retirement planning and lifestyle design and none of Australia's esteemed professional bodies cover it all.

In Sydney in October 2013 and under cover of my Non-Disclosure Agreement, I briefed a convening of some of the city's prominent practitioners. This included a taxation lawyer, a CPA, a Chartered

Accountant and two Certified Financial Planners of which one held an Australian Financial Services License with some 130 Authorised Representative financial planners (many of whom were also accountants). After about four hours of robust questionning and discussion, the group consensus was that the IP was commercially and legally bullet proof. I also had another taxation lawyer, a partner from Brisbane's largest law firm, admit his fascination etc and yes there are others but I'm not naming names as this is not an inquiry into my integrity.

It's widely held that we accountants are a generally conservative bunch and for a number of reasons the main one being, that we seem to work more for the ATO than for you and by this I mean that we conform to ATO standards in terms of only giving advice that fits in with the Commissioner's views of how the tax law applies because if we don't, our professional indemnity insurance is most unlikely to cover us if we get sued by a disgruntled client. This is not to say of course that I have ever or would ever advise someone to operate beyond the law. By contrast, I insist that my clients work within the law however I have become adept at privately gaining the ATO's cooperation to see things my way and in getting this in writing as compared to what my contemporaries understand of matters I engage in.

The same conservatism basically also applies to financial planners but in addition to the ATO, the Australian Securities and Investment Commission (ASIC), has been known to be very firm in dealing with rogue advisers (and rightly so). Accordingly, advisers are reluctant to push beyond established norms and boundaries.

So all up, it appears to me that no one else knows this "stuff" because:

(a) They are systemically pinned down by their regulatory and professional insurance frameworks to be accordingly too fearful to act and; (b) Regardless of the above, they are too busy to do anything about it.

6 - The System Must Reward You for Smart and Fair Play

Every day, businesses large and small spend money on all sorts of things and in each case they are obligated under the tax laws to substantiate their claims for a deduction by way of the following four measures:

1. There is a genuine connection to pursuing or earning assessable income
2. That money was actually spent on the expenses
3. Valid receipts exist for the outgoings
4. The outgoings weren't for a domestic or private purpose on behalf of the owner or owners

It is, therefore absurd that home based businesses have slipped through the cracks for so long in this regard.

Throughout my research, I spoke with more than one hundred accountants nearly all of whom told me that if a home business operator claimed mortgage interest, that a capital gains tax (CGT), liability would arise at sale and therefore it just wasn't worth it.

Of itself, this raises two questions.

1. Is that correct?
2. If so, is that an important enough reason not to do it?

On the first question, the answer is a resounding no and that's due to the operation of the ATO's "interest deductibility test"… *https://www. ato.gov.au/General/Capital-gains-tax/In-detail/Real-estate/Using-your-home-to-produce-income/?page=2*

On the second, a separate analysis would need to be undertaken as the amount of income tax saved "along the way", could far, far outweigh any assessment at the other end.

In my view, the profession has much to answer for being its clients (people like you), have effectively been robbed blind as those of you already running a home business have certainly paid more tax than required and the rest of you haven't been given the incentive to think about starting one up which means your opportunity to prosper was "snuffed" without you ever knowing.

So yes it's a system at play here because nothing operates in isolation. Real estate and business transactions in particular can be very complex given matters such as stamp duty, GST, CGT, contract law and much more can all be involved. So for example when you're speaking to the lawyer, you're not getting proper tax advice and when speaking with the accountant, you're not getting proper legal advice and this further extends to the real estate agent and/or business broker, the mortgage adviser, the financial planner, the insurance broker, the settlement agent and so on. None of these folk have any hope of pulling it all together for you as they lack the time and resources to get it done right the first time. It's actually a case of the blind leading the blind and where no one really knows what is being overlooked along the way.

This awful truth is what drove me to stop seeing clients for about six years as I dedicated myself to figuring it all out.

All this does however have a very happy ending because I can assure you fully that in working within the existing confines of "the system" i.e. Australia's usual lending, business structuring and practices, property investing, its various laws and the many ATO and other rules that apply to us all and more, that you can definitely play it very, very smart to win the game. By winning, I simply mean that you will fare much better than your neighbours whom by comparison and on an otherwise equal footing perhaps, appear asleep at the wheel as they work for a living, pay tax and then struggle to pay off their homes and fund the rest of their lives with what's left.

By contrast, I will have you making your living, paying heaps of property related expenses that already exist, and then paying tax on what's left meaning you have more with which to fund the rest of your life.

So the only question is "do you want to play smart or not"?

Should the ATO or indeed any other government agency ask you for a "please explain", all you need up your sleeve is a carefully constructed "road map" as based on your particular circumstances. Next and providing you are following this road map, all should end well as no agency of government and no government itself is above the law.

Your "map" should do two things:

1. Spell it all out for you in simple, clear, non-technical terms and;
2. Simultaneously spell it all out for the ATO and others in their own technical language inclusive of appropriate references to the many and various provisions of the several laws they administer.

These laws include the following:

- Taxation Administration Act 1953
- Income Tax Assessment Act 1936
- Income Tax Assessment Act 1997
- Fringe Benefits Tax Assessment Act 1986
- Alienation of Personal Services Income Act 2000
- A New Tax System (Goods And Services Tax) Act 1999
- Corporations Act 2001
- And more!

And for the record, I consider myself Australia's sole expert "map maker".

7 - A Very Powerful Integration and Optimisation Platform

As alluded to, this is not just about money, investing, property, business, tax, wealth creation or lifestyle design, it's about all of it!

As a financial planner, my clients had access to many superb investment platforms as constructed by the major banks and investments houses here in Australia and abroad. These platforms allow for a myriad of investment and insurance combinations and with slick functionality and reporting etc. They also include superannuation and self-managed superannuation options.

What they all lack however is the ability for you to invest into your own home as a part- business asset.

Additionally, none of them offer you any fun being you can't entertain your friends, eat dinner or splash about inside them on a lovely, warm weekend afternoon.

None of us are going to be around forever as indeed life is short!

Think about it!

8 - You're Always Controlling What Happens

Ask any homeowner who has previously rented if being in control was an important consideration in deciding to buy and the answer will almost always be yes.

Ask something similar of any small business owner who had ever previously quit their job and you can expect the same response.

According to the McCrindle Blog (13/03/2014), "Having a 'job for life' no longer exists. The workforce has been undergoing a massive transformation over the last three decades and currently the average Australian stays with their employer just 3 years and 4 months – only a third of the way towards long service leave!

If this plays out in the lifetime of a school leaver today it means they will have 17 separate employers in their lifetime".

(*http://mccrindle.com.au/the-mccrindle-blog/job-security-in-australia-no-longer-job-for-life-or-career-for-life*),

Given we can't control say the weather or the economy to name but two obvious examples, at least in running your own home business, you do control almost everything else and so it's no wonder that it's so attractive.

Frank Genovesi

9 - Lowers the Cost of Home Ownership at Any Purchase Price

In buying a property, you're putting your hand up typically for 25 to 30 years to pay down the mortgage in association with meeting the ongoing operating costs such as utilities, council and water rates and building insurance. Over and above, maintenance and repairs also cost money.

The hard facts are however that you must earn money and pay tax before you can tackle these outgoings.

Regardless of purchase price, by applying the strategies herein, you actually get to pay a lot less for it on the basis that you are using some borrowed money to own it.

To earn a dollar, pay tax and then try to pay off your home loan is what nearly everyone does and frankly, it's hard going.

Clearly it's smarter to earn a dollar, pay at least a chunk of the interest on your home loan and then pay tax on what's left!

Taking this simple approach puts you far ahead of your neighbours and you'll be unlikely to ever look back.

The following can render a home many thousands of dollars per annum "cheaper" to pay off.

- Corner blocks with second driveways
- Driveways that flow through to the rear of a property
- Sheds and garages
- Additional parking and garaging space
- Spare bedrooms

- Theatre rooms
- Games rooms
- Formal lounges
- Formal dining rooms
- Family rooms
- Sleep Outs & Enclosed patios
- Parent's and teenager's retreats
- Granny flats
- Balconies and verandah's
- and more.

Accordingly, you effectively get to own your home at a much lower true cost.

The extent to which this is made possible is by a combination of the following factors as broken into two equally important groups:

What's in your own heart and head

As I said before, life is indeed short and it can be taken from us in the blink of an eye so at some time surely you have to ask yourself what makes you happy?

I can't answer that for you but I'm betting it's any combination of the following and in no particular order:

- Love and respect for yourself
- Love and respect for your partner, children and family and knowing they're happy, safe and secure
- A loving partner
- Having a life's purpose
- Good friends to cherish and spend time with
- Leisure
- Honest belief that you are deserving and capable of having of a better life
- Creativity
- Cleverness
- Brilliance

- º Persistence
- º Work ethic
- º Openness and willingness to try new things
- º A willingness to conquer your fears
- º An overwhelming positive versus negative attitude to life
- º Refusing to listen to those who have never done it and don't know how to do it
- º Blocking-out the voices of self-doubt in your own mind
- º A nice home
- º Financial security
- º Travel
- º Interesting, inspiring and rewarding work
- º Ideal work-life balance

You get it I'm sure!

Don't ever forget that the first thing you see in the morning and the last thing you see at night is your home and so it is probably the largest single physical thing in your life and which I suspect made your list.

A smart home business strategy can also help you to tick off the last five things on the above list.

I also strongly believe you're reading this because like many others, you share a burning desire to live well and that your home is the highest measure of that because it fills you with satisfaction and pride of place in this world.

What Does Your Current or Proposed Property Offer?

- º The property floor plan
- º The capability/practicality of the property being modified
- º The layout of the dwelling and other structures on the block of land
- º The property zoning
- º The size of landholding

This is a very exciting concept and once well-grasped, I expect that you will never see property the same way again!

10 - Appropriate Business Structures

Whilst a small business entity can be a sole trader, partnership, company or trust, to benefit from all this, going forward, an appropriate business structure needs to be ascertained in accordance with your personal and business needs and situations.

Hence and if you're already in business and likely to derive a future capital gain from the sale of your business assets (most likely business premises and/or business goodwill), you should now carefully examine your options.

If on the other hand you're considering entering into business, please consider the potential for creating future capital gains (again as most likely to come from an increase in the capital value of your yet to be purchased business premises and/or business goodwill). As such, it's smart to determine an appropriate business structure now.

And should business go well for you, prime considerations are the amount of income tax you are already paying and may also need to pay in future.

Proprietary Limited Companies (Pty Ltd)

These work because a company can be recorded on a Certificate of Title as a Tenant In Common with other owners as it stands as a separate legal entity from its shareholders and it can own real property.

Sole Traders

Only natural persons can be sole traders (also known as sole proprietorships). Accordingly, they can also own real property to live in and work from. This is also an acceptable business structure.

Partnerships

Partnerships arise from sole traders having "banded together" to own a business. If the partnership doesn't consist of a married or de-facto couple living together, then to make it work for these purposes, at least one partner must live and work from the subject property.

Limited Companies (Ltd)

Generally speaking, these are large companies listed on the stock exchange which often have a net value that exceeds $6M and this is problematic in this context. In any case, the shareholders are many and these cannot possibly co-habit residential properties in the manner as required by the strategies to be therefore unsuitable.

Trusts

There are many types of trusts e.g. family trusts, non-fixed trusts, fixed unit trusts, discretionary trusts, hybrid trusts, service trusts, public unit trusts, testamentary (will) trusts, superannuation trusts and so on. However and unfortunately, they are incapable of owning real property assets and hence the difficulty lies with the fact that a trust cannot therefore appear on the Certificate of Title for a home business property. It may be possible to circumvent this by having the business assets owned by a trust with a corporate trustee (normally a related private company), which is responsible for the trading activities of the trust (and of course after having appropriately amended or prepared a new trust deed).

Co-operatives

These are unsuited to the "SBRB" and for the same reasons as outlined above at sole traders and partnerships generally because they are not designed to provide a return on investment including distribution of profits to members.

11 - What Is A Business?

To merit an undertaking of the "SBRB", we must understand that according to the Australian Taxation Office (ATO), there's no simple answer to this question so the more of the following that you can evidence in your favour when considered in combination and as a whole, then the more likely it is that you are carrying on a business.

- Is there repetition and regularity to your activity?
- Do you have a purpose of profit as well as a prospect of profit?
- Does your activity have a significant commercial purpose or character?
- Do you have more than just an intention to engage in business?
- Is your activity planned, organised and carried on in a business-like manner?
- Is your activity carried on in a similar manner to other businesses in your industry?
- Is it fair to say the activity is more a business, rather than a hobby, recreation or sporting activity?
- Does your activity have characteristics of size, scale and permanency?

All this matters because any money you receive from the activity will be treated as assessable income plus; you'll be entitled to an Australian business number (ABN) as well as registering for the Goods and Services Tax (GST), which in some cases you must.

The sort of business you conduct is wide-open for you to explore. You could perhaps try tutoring, arts and craft, setting yourself up with an online business or in pursuing your trade or profession. The possibilities are endless as it's really about whatever takes your fancy in concert with whatever you think can be commercially worthwhile.

Remember that in tax matters; any allowable expenses you incur in earning this income are generally entitled to be claimed as tax deductions and if you lose money, depending on your business structure, you may be entitled to offset this loss against other income or to carry it forward to offset against future income to reduce the income tax you might have to pay in the future.

What if it's really just a hobby?

Firstly, this needs to be determined by the surrounding facts as money you earn from this activity is generally not assessable income so you can't claim any tax deductions in relation thereto. You also can't carry forward any losses you might make into other tax years nor reduce your current year's income by way of offset.

How can I prove that I'm running a business?

Again, there's no magic bullet but once again in terms of the following, the more the merrier:

- You've invested time and money into setting it up
- You prepared a business plan
- You've advertised
- You've done your market research
- You've logged ongoing time expended, meetings and/or kept other relevant entries
- You use your existing qualifications, knowledge, skills and experience
- Etc ...

12 - What Is A Small Business?

Once you've established that you're carrying on a business and that your activities aren't merely an interest or a hobby, for the sake of utilising a home business strategy, it must be a "small business" that is, one that passes a number of fairly easy ATO tests.

In order to benefit from implementing the contents of this book, you or your business and related entities must not own assets with a total net value of more than six million dollars and you also need to keep turnover to less than two million dollars per annum. Unless you manage to stay within those limits, you'll have some happy problems to sort out so you might want to contact me or someone else for specialist tax advice.

It's also important that you run your home business for at least half the time you own the property (i.e. if less than 15 years) or at least seven and a half years if more than 15 years.

I anticipate most readers fitting these criteria.

13 - Tax Stuff In More Detail

Ah yes … and now to follow are seven lucky do's and do not's in what is our special lucky chapter number 13!

Presuming you are following the law correctly, as you work your home business strategy, you should expect the following:

1. When using a company, capital gains tax (CGT) does NOT apply to any capital growth of the private & domestic component of the property (i.e. your main residence).
2. In using a company, Fringe Benefits Tax (FBT) does NOT apply to the employer company.
3. The anti-avoidance provisions of what is arguably the most draconian piece of Australian Commonwealth taxation legislation ever to have existed do NOT apply (i.e. the very much feared Part IVA of the ITAA 1997).
4. Many superior ongoing taxation deductions DO apply compared to "usual" home office situations, where one has an alternative place of business to their home.
5. Superior building depreciation allowances DO apply versus "usual" home office situations, where one has an alternative place of business to their home.
6. CGT does NOT apply in respect of the ATO's own Interest Deductibility Test.
7. Reduced or Nil, state government land tax to pay DOES apply.

Land Tax

Whilst varied in scale and application across different Australian states and territories, land tax is generally payable on all non-exempt property.

The general rule seems to be that as long as the owners live in the house whilst running any one or more businesses as a sole trader or perhaps in a typical husband and wife style partnership that an exemption exists. However where the property is newly constructed or refurbished, it may not.

Note that when a company exists on the title and uses its interest to operate a business, its director/s and shareholder/s (who would be normally living in the home), is/are supposed to apply to the relevant authority for a partial exemption for the personal use areas by describing the situation including the extent of the business use and subsequent financial interest (and to prove this), so correct assessments can be issued thus including a taxable component commensurate to the company's interest. When you look at the numbers holistically however, this is not a major impost and certainly not a deal-breaker.

Interest deductibility test

We made the case earlier that for whatever reason, it appears no one has thought much about this before (hey the world used to be flat — remember)?

It unfortunately appears to me that thousands of Australians have been incorrectly advised by their accountants to NOT claim the relevant proportion of mortgage interest, council rates and building insurance (i.e. occupancy expenses), instead to just claim some extra heating and lighting etc (i.e. running expenses), so as to legally side-step any capital gains tax (CGT) liability at future sale. Well the very bad news is that for years, The ATO have had a little something up their sleeve called the "Interest Deductibility Test". This means that if your home has been used to produce income (e.g. rent from a spare bedroom) or it has an area that has been exclusively or almost exclusively set aside as a place of business (e.g. office, studio, workshop etc) and if any such area or areas have the character of a place of business, then CGT will always apply as The ATO looks to see if you could have borrowed money and claimed the interest costs, not whether or not you actually did (oh and your borrowing capacity throughout the period is immaterial)!

CGT main residence exemption

In general, your entitlement to the full capital gains tax, main residence exemption is diluted to whatever extent that you use your home to earn assessable income.

To be clear, I'm not saying your home will be CGT free upon disposal, only that irrespective of your business structure and despite whatever CGT liability may arise by having passed the interest deductibility test (as just explained above), that various provisions exist within the tax law for you to reduce the liability or to even wipe it out altogether.

Alienation of personal services income

Since 1st July 2000, under The New Business Tax System (Alienation of Personal Services Income) Act 2000, each of partnerships, companies and trusts have needed to meet one or more of four particular tests to determine whether or not they are running a "Personal Services Business". This matters here as in order for you to achieve the best results in terms of wealth creation and lifestyle enhancement, instead of as a sole trader, your home business may operate under a partnership, private company structure or as a Discretionary Family Trust with a Corporate trustee.

The Act is all about ensuring that contractors and consultants who mainly personally produce income, do not "off-load" some of it to others for the purpose of paying less tax.

If personal services income is channelled through a company, partnership or trust (a personal services entity), it is still the individual's personal services income for income tax purposes.

The changes to the tax law only apply to personal services income, not to personal services businesses.

In figuring it all out, there are four steps to potentially work through:

Step 1: Have You Received PSI?

Like I said, not if you qualify as a personal services business hence, you'll need to meet the results test plus ensure that less than 80 per cent of your personal services income in an income year comes from each client and you'll need to meet one of the other three personal services business tests (i.e. the unrelated clients test, employment test or business premises test) or you can obtain a determination from the Tax Office confirming that you are running a personal services business.

If you qualify, the legislation doesn't apply to you. To determine whether or not this is the case, there are a number of rules and tests to observe:

Step 2: The Results Test:

If you earn personal services income, you will meet the results test in the income year if, in respect of at least 75% of this income, you can answer YES TO ALL THREE of the following questions about your work.

1. Under your contract or arrangement, is the personal services income paid to achieve a specified result or outcome?
2. Do you have to provide the tools or equipment necessary (if any) to do your work? (If no tools or equipment are required, answer YES.)
3. Are you liable for rectifying defects in your work?

Step 3: The 80 Percent Rule:

If you don't meet the results test and 80 percent or more of your personal services income in the income year comes from one client, you cannot self-assess whether you meet the other tests at step four (4). The changes to the tax law apply to you unless you get a determination from the Tax Office.

If you don't meet the results test, you can self-assess against the other tests at step four (4) if less than 80% of your personal services income comes from each client.

Step 4: The Remaining Tests

The Unrelated Clients Test: Does the individual doing the personal services work have personal services income from two or more clients who are not associated with each other or with you (or the individual, if you are a personal services entity)?

The Employment Test: Do you have employees or engage sub-contractors or entities who perform at least 20% (by market value) of the principal work?

The Business Use Test: You'll meet this one providing that at all times throughout an income year, you rightfully occupy and use the premises in each of the manners as follows:

- It is owned or leased by you
- It is mainly used to conduct the work (that is, more than 50% of the use) from which the personal services income is gained or produced
- It is used exclusively by you
- It is physically separate from the business address of your clients, or their associates
- It is physically separate from the private residence of the individual doing the personal services work, or their associates

From this, it's apparent how the business use test will be difficult to meet if you operate in a home that does not have a physically separate area with dedicated entry etc. Consequently, if you choose to rely on this test, you'll need to carefully consider the style and layout of a particular property for your home-based business. Most people should find that meeting the results test, the 80% Rule and the Unrelated Clients Test will be the easiest way to qualify as a Personal Services Business but of course, everyone's own circumstances will be the determinant.

Non-commercial losses

As a sole trader or partner in a partnership, you can deduct your home business losses from other assessable income (e.g. your main and/or secondary employment, investment earnings, another business in your name etc), unless you are prohibited by the application of the non-commercial loss rules in which case, you can still defer those losses indefinitely for application towards income from a future year or years (similar to how companies carry their losses forward).

In order to claim a loss, you must earn less than $250,000 per annum from any combination of the following sources:

1. Total net investment losses - including financial investment losses and rental property losses (these are added back to your other income as with Centrelink's income calculation policy)
2. Reportable superannuation contributions
3. Taxable income (ignoring any business losses)
4. Total reportable fringe benefits

You must also pass one of the following four tests:

1. You continually use non-real property assets worth at least $100,000 in the business
2. Three out of the past five years (including the current year) have produced a profit
3. At least $500,000 of real property or an interest in real property is continually used in the business
4. At least $20,000 of assessable income has been produced from the business

Considering that for every dollar you earn from your "normal job", if you were to set aside the right amount of space for your home business such that the deductions you could legally claim equalled your income from that job, then providing you meet the non-commercial loss requirements as laid out above, you'd be earning a tax free annual income of anything up to $250,000 as depending on your circumstances (or otherwise a substantially tax free income due to the first $20,000 that would remain taxable in order to pass the last test above but only if absolutely necessary).

I think this is pretty cool and hope you're ok with yanking this much joy from the system!

14 - To Build Or To Buy Established? – That Is The Question!

A matter of Personal Choice

First and foremost, because 'lifestyle' is such a huge part of what the SBRB is about, one must personally consider which would make them "happier" because we're not just talking about money here!

Some folk prefer older homes of character and distinction whilst others love the modern and/or funky vibe – there's no right or wrong.

Of course, when building, you can choose a design that suits your needs rather than trying to make an existing property fit with your needs.

Building Depreciation

New buildings will always provide better taxation write-downs than older ones as they have had no "effective life" used up as yet. Older buildings which have been extended or substantially improved however, may still provide substantial depreciation benefits to the extent of the money expended on those capital works. It is also very important to understand the difference between repairs that are usually tax deductible as expenses in the year incurred (on assessable income-producing properties), versus a capital cost, which is written-down over the effective life of the capital improvement.

(Note): In claiming depreciation expenses on the home business proportion of your home, the cost base to assess any future capital gains tax (CGT) liability at sale reduces by the total of the amounts claimed. However, as our Procedures potentially allow for no CGT to be paid anyway, this doesn't present as much of a disadvantage if any.

Improvement Value

It is certainly arguable that building a house on an empty block can add more to the overall end- value than the individual summed-cost of the building contract and the land. As always though, research and compare.

15 - A Buffer Against Some Negative Forces In The Economy

Paying your home's expenses significantly with untaxed money is of itself, a buffer against the following:

- ○ Interest rate rises (e.g. a 0.25% rate rise = just 0.175% @ a 30% marginal tax rate)
- ○ Inflation (e.g. rising council and water rates, repairs, maintenance etc @ CPI of say 3% = only 2.1% @ a 30% marginal tax rate)
- ○ Rising house prices (when looking to buy)
- ○ Obtaining GST credits on purchases made in connection with the business use percentage of the property.

16 - Help Yourself To A Cost-Effective Home Upgrade

After thinking this through, you may decide to sell your home and to buy another that you consider nicer and better located or that is in any other one or more ways superior.

In so doing, you know of course that this will likely cost you more money but you are comforted by your new-found knowledge of the fact that the system helps you fund it to the extent it is used to run a business.

In say taking on any amount of further debt to buy a great property as better suited to the dual purpose, well staged, you should expect significant extra deductions for interest on the new debt.

You might even find your situation supports a restructure of your business to effect a FULL tax deduction for the interest incurred on the new debt.

Taking it even further, a smartly planned move can effect FULL deductibility of the loan interest for both the existing debt and the new debt!

17 - How About A Cost-Effective Home Extension?

It may well be that you're already living in what you feel is a really nice home and or in a great street and or in a great suburb and if so then good for you however none of this necessarily means that your current home-sweet-home is even remotely suited to an effective home business strategy!

To hit the mark, every property needs to get two things right:

1. Be large enough to comfortably cater to the dual purpose and;
2. Have a great floor plan and flow etc, thus to ensure the deductions are potent.

Getting it right allows the following to be achievable:

º The interest on the borrowings to construct the addition can be fully deductible regardless of whether or not the extensions are put to business use (e.g. a $200,000 extension at an interest cost of 5% p.a. is worth $10,000 p.a in deductions)

º Division 43 of the ITAA 1997 provides for a system of deducting capital expenditure incurred in the construction of building and other capital works. Allowable deductions may be able to be claimed at 2.5% of the construction cost for the next 40 years (e.g. a $200,000 extension is worth another $5,000 p.a in deductions).

So before you have plans drawn up, it's worth thinking this through very carefully!

All up, don't be surprised when you start seriously thinking about extending your existing, much loved home to make it the ever more ideal home business property.

These days, a granny flat strategy has found significant appeal in the community as a means to house aging parents, teenagers or even an "airbnb" style income earning proposition. Of course, an extension to your home to accommodate a home business strategy can also be designed with this in mind for the future just in case the home business doesn't work out for any reason or if life take an unexpected turn.

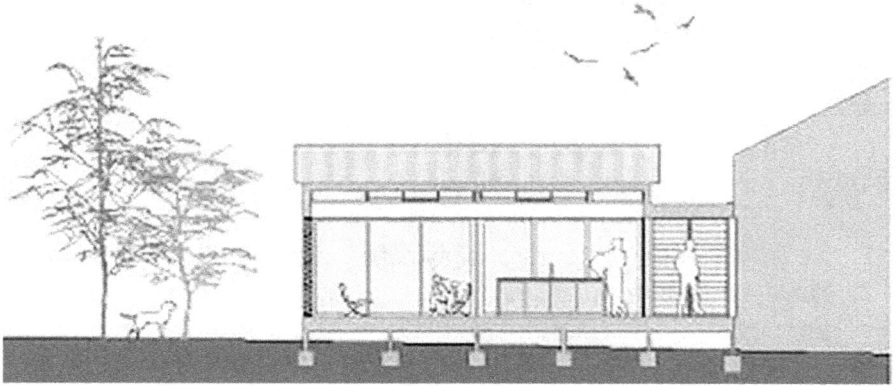

18 - Wipe Out Some Or All Of Your Existing Personal Debt

As you probably know, at law, companies are separate to their shareholders (i.e. their owners).

This means that a home business run by a sole trader or perhaps a husband and wife partnership has certain different characteristics to one as run under a private company structure.

From the perspective of the tax deductibility of the mortgage, a company's share of that debt is calculated with reference to its financial interest as noted on the title to the security property (in this case, your home).

Example:

$500,000 Property value

$300,000 Mortgage

66.66% Loan to value ratio (LVR)

40% Company's financial interest

40% Business Use Percentage of the property (BUP)

In the above example and despite an LVR that exceeds the BUP, the full $300,000 loan is nonetheless a business loan and therefore can be wholly deductible. However in so claiming the additional deductions for the extent of attributed debt between 40 and 66.66 percent, the company would incur a housing fringe benefit tax liability which must be factored. In this respect, it is wise to match the business use percentage to the financial deductions percentage of the mortgage interest as to be claimed. Hence in this example, I'd suggest limiting the deduction to 40 percent.

It's worth doing the sums and broadly considering a range of matters to determine whether or not a company business structure is appropriate.

Considerations include:

- Income Tax
- Loss of the CGT 50 percent discount on disposal (this is not the end of the world though as there are many ways to eat the cherry on this cake)
- Asset protection
- And more

19 - Give Or Grab A Leg-Up Into Home Ownership

The Co-Owners Wealth Builder (COWB).

It allows people to band together to buy a home in which at least one them will live and from where either separately or together, a business is commenced and operated.

It typically suits those renting or living with family or friends.

For Parents and Their Adult Children

Using a company:

These days, commercial lenders have tightened their criteria in demanding higher deposits and so it's clear that many young adults will struggle to save a deposit for their first home. The COWB can help parents step in to ensure their children secure a loan and which simultaneously does the following:

1. It assists them into a home of their own
2. It keeps them from renting (so as to be both a roof over their head and a place of business), finally kick-starting the journey to building some equity of their own and;
3. It allows the parents to get their "personal space" back as otherwise these sons and daughters may continue to live at home for a lot longer than anyone really expected or dare I say wanted (and surely that's for some)

The idea is for the parent/s to help their kids to obtain a loan to buy a good house in a good area where he or she can live and work, by operating a home-based business. Parent/s will also require an ownership interest in the property by way of a shareholding in the private company that holds an interest on the title (as tenant in common with their adult child or children).

This unique arrangement affords the following benefits:

º It provides bricks and mortar security to the shareholder/parents because the loan they've undoubtedly had to guarantee to the lender will usually be for less than the value of the property and typically at 80% loan to value ratio. Of course property values can decline in the short term and if the loan was to be called in, the parent could have capital at risk if it were sold for less than the outstanding loan balance, so they'd be properly advised by the lender to take independent legal advice in this and other associated regards

º The parents and their children must both agree on what type of business is to be run. This brings up the opportunity for the parent to assist the business in any capacity that is agreed between the parties. Typically, the parent becomes either a working Director or is otherwise employed by the company whereby they impart pearls of wisdom or other benefits from their years of knowledge and experience to help ensure the success of the business

º It allows the parties to be closely involved in a business enterprise and if managed well, this can add that special something to the inter-personal relationships at play. However, it could go the other way but it's important to acknowledge that the ownership "structure" does not of itself have the capacity to influence people's behaviour or attitude. It serves only to accommodate a hopeful willingness to cooperate under our proprietary "Joint Property Sharing Agreement" inclusive of the associated business arrangements

º Whatever the financial contribution to the property as made by the parent or parents, the child's home loan stands to be repaid more quickly if a profitable business is run

º The embedded cost and tax savings in running a home-based business (i.e. as contrary to parents helping their sons or daughters to run a business from separate premises), assists the business'

cash-flow and growth
º Superior quality of accommodation and location afforded by the parent's help in comparison to whatever the child may have been able to achieve without that help as further coupled with other advantages inherent to running a home business, means the long-term financial outlook for holding the property is considerably better than under any other ownership structure

Doing this in a partnership:

Conceptually, it is similar to the above with the essential difference being the parent and child form a business partnership and the parent helps the child buy their first home either in the child's own name or jointly (howsoever they might agree) and where the business is run from one or more dedicated business use areas within the child's home. Either way the parent can lodge a caveat on the title to protect their interest and have a solicitor draw up an agreement to cover matters beyond the scope of the template "Joint Property Sworn Statement" which I developed and can be made available.

For siblings and/or very close friends – a variation on the COWB (i)

The above thinking can be equally applied to siblings and/or very close friends who think they can communicate and deal with each other at all the various levels required to successfully walk this path. It all boils down to trust, love and caring about each other to the point that you're willing to do something truly wonderful for someone else and in the process, get something good out of it for yourself.

E.g. Dan has an average paying job without great prospects and he doesn't have much money. He also currently rents a room in his brother Don's house. What he does have in his favour though, is a really good business idea that he's busting to try out.

Don, on the other hand, has a steady job in IT and earns an above average income. They discuss at great lengths the merits of Dan's business idea and agree that by working together, it can work and better yet, Don thinks he can set up and manage all the IT requirements for much less than if Dan went elsewhere for that side of things and that these aspects would be a big driver to their success.

The arrangement could go like this then:

1. Don is willing to help Dan by;
   Applying for a joint loan with Dan to buy a property they have in mind. Putting down a 20% deposit (obtained say from his home equity) By including his income into the lender's loan affordability calculations and; in guaranteeing all Dan's obligations under the loan contract (as probably required by the lender).
2. They set up a new private company that we'll call D & D Pty Ltd. However, because the lender wouldn't make a loan to it to buy its interest in the property (because it didn't have any trading figures), D & D Pty Ltd enters into a commercial loan agreement with Dan and/or Don as its shareholders, to borrow the money from them with which to purchase its share of floor space to be set aside for its exclusive business use within the property (remembering that Dan and Don have just borrowed this very money and more from the commercial lender to buy the property). With this loan in place from its shareholders, D & D Pty Ltd now pays each of them for its appropriate financial interest in the property.
3. Dan and Don now pay their respective half shares of this sum off of their personal share of the mortgage on the property (in Dan's case) and of Don's personal mortgage on his home (remembering that he put down a 20% deposit out of his home equity). Thus in each case, they've reduced or even eliminated their non-tax deductible debt in this regard (awesome)!
4. D & D Pty Ltd now has a tax-deductible business loan (i.e; the interest component) that it should repay Dan and Don (as its shareholders), every week, fortnight or month or even just in one repayment per annum (it doesn't matter at this point).
5. Dan and Don now must treat the interest component from any business loan repayments they receive from D & D Pty Ltd, as part of their personal taxable income.

6. Also, by agreement with Dan, Don is employed either as a working Director or otherwise by the company and remains at all times, an equal shareholder with Dan in the company. (Note); if they preferred, Don wouldn't work for the company at all and instead he'd simply own a shareholding in the company whilst Dan ran the business by himself in which case, the company might simply pay Don upon receiving his Tax Invoices (i.e. as just another supplier to it in respect of his IT services and where obviously Don would need to obtain his own ABN in that case).

Issues

Now in either case (i.e. parent/children or siblings/friends), the day may well come when someone wants to sell the property to extract their share of the money so let's take a look:

1. If the person who helped out the other by guaranteeing their loan wants to end the arrangement, then the beneficiary of that help must be able to pay out the other's shareholding in the company (as measured by its assets less its liabilities). In a simple scenario, we'd be at least looking at the relevant share of any equity the company had in the property. The problem could be that the recipient of the help might still not be financially able to do that and so the provider of the help would have to convince them to sell the property (knowing that they'd also be selling their home out from under them), possibly causing an awful strain on the relationship. Hence, before going down this path, the parties would be wise to write down their worst case/nightmare scenarios and to discuss and agree on what courses they would be willing to adopt and to then have a lawyer draft an agreement to preserve the arrangement in the form of a legally binding deed to be duly executed and independently witnessed. In this manner, any disputes can be resolved by referring to the agreement if necessary. To conserve solicitor costs, such provisions can be drafted into the already mandatory "Joint Property Sharing Agreement".
2. If it's the recipient of the help who "wants out" of the property, then the "provider" may not be all too happy if he or she has

invested significant time, energy or money into the business, especially if the recipient is unwilling to continue in the business. This is because although the property may sell for enough to repay all its secured loans, the business itself may not survive the separation of its owners or it doesn't have sufficient maturity of its own accord, to be sold with any worthwhile component of goodwill.

In either case above, we are referring to matters that all co-owners of privately held businesses must responsibly consider and deal with in advance if they do not wish to face such situations unprepared.

The COWB (ii)

Stay In One Party's Current Purchased Home For All To Live In & From Where to Start a Business.

Staying with Dan and Don, here's a different scenario to ponder:

1. Dan wants to buy his first home but he doesn't have a sufficient deposit or borrowing power to buy anything all that great.
2. Don on the other hand, has $200,000 of equity in a home that is suitable for dual use and worth $500,000.
3. Dan still wants to start up a business based on the good idea as previously referred.
4. Don may or may not want to be involved in running the business (it doesn't matter).
5. Don is happy for Dan to move in to live (or to perhaps keep living there if already already doing so) and to also operate one or more businesses (either by himself or together), from the spare room/s.
6. Neither of them want to get married and start a family in the foreseeable future.
7. They form a company D & D Pty Ltd, that will use 30% of the floor space and which will contribute 30% of the capital (i.e; $500,000 x 0.3 = $150,000).
8. Dan's total financial contribution limit is $150,000 so from the $500,000 purchase price, Don gets the balance in his name i.e;

$500,000 Total
- $150,000 D & D Pty Ltd
- $150,000 Dan
= $200,000 Don

(Note): In keeping the above example simple, we have not accounted for the fact that stamp duty is payable on the transfers of land to D & D Pty Ltd as well as to Dan hence the amounts of financial interests relative to the parties would likely need to be adjusted in line with everyone's capacity unless some other arrangement was made.

9. They'll seek independent legal advice and mutually agree to incorporate such into the template JPSA to cover their personal relationship and obligations as pertaining to the property.

The COWB (iii)

Extend One Party's Home For All To Live In & From Where To Start a Business

To illustrate, we'll go back to Dan and Don and imagine a new scenario:

1. Dan wants to start up a business based on the good idea as previously referred.
2. Don wants to be involved in the business.
3. Dan wants to buy his first home but he doesn't have a sufficient deposit or borrowing power to buy anything particularly good.
4. Don has a nice home but it's too small for them both to live in and for the business to be run from there.
5. They both think for at least the next 5 years they won't be very interested in getting married and starting a family.
6. They like the idea of building an extension to Don's house to make it large enough to allow a suitable business operation of their choice and so they can both live there as well.
7. Dan is happy to financially contribute to the value of 50% of the contract price of the extensions and in return, Don agrees to

Dan being an equal shareholder in D & D Pty Ltd that will hold an interest on the title as tenant in common.

8. Dan also wants to buy into Don's personal share of the house because he doesn't want to rent and Don doesn't mind because he can use the money (tax free from the partial sale of his main residence as he has never used it to earn income), to pay out his mortgage to be personally debt free.

9. Hence; all the parties i.e; Dan, Don and their proposed company will become tenants in common.

10. For future CGT substantiation purposes (and to save arguments), Don has his house currently professionally valued at say $500,000 by a licensed valuer and Dan agrees to buy say a 25% interest for $125,000.

11. The cost of the building extension is quoted at $210,000.

12. They agree that the improved value for CGT purposes will be $700,000 and that as D & D Pty Ltd will occupy some 30% of the floor space, then as 30% of the value of the home equals $210,000, that it's a great match.

13. onsidering that D & D Pty Ltd will have a 30% interest in the property (half each to Dan and Don as shareholders) and that Dan will have a 25% interest, Don will therefore hold a 45% interest.

14. They will seek independent legal advice and mutually agree to incorporate such into the template JPSA to cover their personal relationship and obligations as pertaining to the property.

The COWB (iv)

Upgrade One Party's Home For All To Live In & From Where To Start a Business.

Staying with Dan and Don and imagining again a further new scenario:

1. Don has a nice home worth $500,000 with $200,000 in equity and wants to upgrade into a better home in a better area.

2. Dan wants to buy his first home but he doesn't have a sufficient deposit or borrowing power to buy anything that great.

3. Dan wants to start up a business based on the good idea as

previously referred.

4. Don wants to be involved in the business.
5. Neither of them want to get married and start a family in the foreseeable future.
6. hey've decided on a house that's large enough to allow a suitable business operation of their choice and they want to buy it together at $700,000.
7. Don will sell his home and use the equity as a deposit on their mutual behalf (we'll keep it simple and just say that he and Dan have enough cash to cover the out of pocket expenses associated with selling up and moving).
8. D & D Pty Ltd will use 30% of the floor space and will contribute 30% of the capital (i.e; $700,000 x 0.3 = $210,000).
9. Dan's total financial limit is $250,000 so from the $700,000 purchase price, Don gets the balance in his name i.e;

$700,000 Total
$210,000 D & P/L
$250,000 Dan
=$240,000 Don

10. Remember now that Don has only $200,000 in equity so either he borrows an extra $40,000 in his own name or the lads will need to rethink the numbers and of course it doesn't matter whether they buy something less expensive, or if Don does take out that extra loan or if Dan buys a lesser percentage in his own name because it's a just fictitious example, solely to illustrate how to start thinking in this way.
11. hey'll apply for a joint loan for the balance of the replacement property's purchase price.
12. They'll determine the relevant ownership interests.
13. They'll seek independent legal advice and mutually agree to incorporate such into the template JPSA to cover their personal relationship and obligations as pertaining to the property.

In respect of all of the above scenarios (i.e The COWB (i) – (iv) inclusive, a sole trader and/or partnership business structure could be used instead of a company and if so, references to Joint Property Sharing Agreements must be replaced with Joint Property Sworn Statements.

Consider for example that a home might have four bedrooms and some formal areas and that Dan and Don would typically occupy a bedroom each for private use and share the kitchen, laundry and lounge or family room etc.

Here goes:

1. They could use one spare bedroom each to run their own businesses as sole traders or;
2. The two spare bedrooms could be used by a partnership that might exist or;
3. here could be one sole trader and one partnership in existence using one room each or;
4. There could be two sole traders occupying a spare bedroom each and a partnership occupying one or two formal rooms.

Can you think of any others?

How about Jane and Jim, a married or de-facto couple living together in a similar property:

1. They sleep together in the master bedroom and use the ensuite and/or;
2. One of their parents also runs a business with them in partnership (from a spare bedroom or two) and/or;
3. One of them runs a business as a sole trader from another spare bedroom and/or;
4. The couple run a different business in partnership from the formal lounge and dining.

Of course all along we could refer to garages and back sheds as business use areas instead of or in addition to the internal rooms to the home.

And so it goes etc ...

Better than The Federal Government's First Home Owners Grant

Absolutely!

The FHOG is a once-off payment of $10,000 to buy a newly constructed home.

Whilst it certainly helps with gathering a deposit, it does nothing more and it is regularly commented upon in the media that the property sector most frequented for the FHOG is largely artificially price-inflated as a result so this begs whether or not is represents its "full value".

IMPORTANT: The rules surrounding the FHOG disqualify anyone from obtaining it if they wish for a private company to co-exist on the title (as only individuals who have not previously owned their own home may band together to share one grant). Once you get over this however, a bigger and better picture emerges. As such, it's one or the other – that's the decision that needs to be made!

Depending on the size of the loan taken out to buy a suitable property, in addition to other deductible business property expenses, the COWB can save a few thousand dollars or more in tax (EVERY YEAR), for any profitable business that operates from the property (and as we know, company tax losses can be carried forward and used in future years).

In contrast to the FHOG, there is no cap on the purchase price of the property so this means and depending on individual circumstances, that some may be able to purchase higher quality properties in better locations and set themselves up for better long-term capital growth. This aspect alone could be worth hundreds of thousands of dollars over the course of one's lifetime.

It's easy to see that it won't take long for the regular savings to overtake a once-off gift.

If however, it is ultimately decided to use the "COWB" under a business partnership arrangement, then providing the parent has never owned a home in Australia, they could buy the property with their child and share the FHOG.

Alternatively, if the parents have ever owned a home in Australia and they are comfortable in NOT having their name on the Certificate Of Title, the child could still apply for the FHOG.

20 - Big, Free Money

Saves Doubled-Up Property Expenses

Compared to the traditional setting of commercial premises, a home business set up allows you to obliterate all of the following recurring expenses:

- No travel to and from work which means a decline in motor vehicle wear and tear with corresponding lowered maintenance costs, less fuel consumption, a higher resale value due to lower kilometres and for some, no parking fees.
- No monthly lease payments for business premises.
- Lower business fire and general insurance premiums.
- No separate electricity, gas and water supply charges.
- No or lower staff wages to pay.
- No staff amenities to provide.
- No need for expensive phone systems, photocopiers, complicated computer networks, etc
- No Land Tax to pay if private share of rateable value falls below minimum threshold.
- No mortgage interest to pay if buying the premises

The following represents the annual savings from one of my past operations way back in 2002:

- $ 40,000   Business premises lease, management fees & outgoings
- $ 3,000   Motor vehicle running expenses, commuting to and from work
- $ 5,000   Business property and related insurances
- $ 70,000   Staff salaries
- $ 6,300   Compulsory superannuation on salaries
- $ 1,000   Staff amenities

- º $ 3,600   Lease payments on office equipment
- º **$128,900**   **Total Gross Savings**

Typically, a home business has all of these expenses except for say staff related ones which amount in the above case to $77,300. The other $51,600 however are pure savings and all without really "going without". Furthermore and very importantly, all similar existing private expenses that will change their characteristic to business expenses via the connection to running a home business, will still be deductible for tax purposes so it's a win with lower costs coupled with a no-loss on deductions scenario!

Invest or Reinvest Business Cost Savings

Whilst everyone's savings will be different due to the uniqueness of individual businesses, the point remains the same for all by imagining what your business could do with the extra cash.

E.g. Fund a program of external investment or business growth, thus potentially growing the benefits over time.

Pay Yourself More

Alternatively, instead of expansion or investment and depending on your business structure, why not pay yourself additional personal income via higher salary, dividends or distributions. Ok so this would be taxable but it's still better than having unnecessarily higher expenses and not receiving additional income!

Invest Income Tax Savings

Just in claiming annual business expense and building depreciation tax deductions for the business portion of ownership should yield the average home business many thousands every year in tax savings. Extrapolated over say one, two or three decades, we are talking BIG money. E.g. a $5000 annual tax saving invested at 7% net return (even excluding indexation), could return $316,000 over 25 years.

Alternatively, those savings can be put to many good uses by the business (for example):

- Reduce debt (as arguably it's another form of saving).
- Create additional income through advertising etc.
- Improve existing assets.
- Purchase new assets

Invest CGT Savings

Imagine if in say 10 years from now you were to sell your home business for a capital gain of say $400,000 and further presuming you were very switched-on in knowing how to account for the proceeds such that you paid no capital gains tax (this is very do-able in many, many circumstances), then you could most reasonably presume that the tax you saved would be significant. So keeping it simple, let's go with say a 30% tax rate which equals $120,000.

If you then invested that same $120,000 and managed to receive average growth of around seven percent per annum, it would almost double in value every 10 years.

So let's say you're 30 years old now and that this happens to you when you're 40. In that case, you'd have $120,000 available to invest and which you might not cash in until you're retired at say 65 years old meaning that over the next 25 years, your $120,000 turns into $687,000.

Of course there are many variations and variables but no doubt you get the idea and I'm betting that you agree that $687,000 is a heck of a free kick in life.

Sell What Your Business No Longer Needs

Should you have any existing small business assets that you don't really want or need in future, certain rules allow you to sell them and disregard any capital gains assessment as long as you replace them within two years and use or have them ready for use in your business.

This strategy lets you boost the deposit on your next home by using untaxed money from the sale of these assets. Consider that if you sold an active business asset for say a $300,000 assessable capital gain but had your act together enough to save yourself say $90,000 in capital gains tax, you'd be beautifully positioned for future growth on that $90,000 for however long it was invested.

So again at over 25 years say and at another 7 percent average annual return, that's another $515,000 out of thin air just waiting for you to grab a hold of!

Of course in the real world property growth rates are not constant and we haven't factored in the costs associated with buying and selling and in transferring assets from say a sole trader or partnership to a company or a trust (if desired), so as to be able to claim the relevant other benefits of that a different business ownership structure. However, and the point is, if you believe that a better location is a main determinant in obtaining superior long-term capital growth from real estate, then spending more money to acquire that location is typically required with the good news being my strategies accommodate this. All the other benefits set aside, the above illustrations are there to simply put some numbers on the page to mathematically illustrate what is possible.

Furthermore, I've NOT even considered here that you're supposed to run a business that should make you some money and that you can get your hands on this as the business owner and use it for personal pleasure, investment or further business growth and expansion etc.

Pay Off Your Home Years Faster For a Guaranteed Rate of Return And Huge Savings On Interest

Generally speaking, paying off any non-deductible component of your home loan is a good way to invest the cost and/or the tax savings because you get a set rate of return i.e. the reverse effect of the interest rate the bank charges you on outstanding loan balances. This is arguably safer than chasing typically fluctuating returns from more speculative investments and it completely negates any risk of a negative return.

E.g. If one my strategies saved you even just $100 per fortnight in tax on a $300,000 mortgage at five percent interest and you regularly paid these savings off your home loan, you would save $49,390 in interest over 25 years and wipe off around four years and nine months from your repayment schedule.

Let Capital Growth On Your Superior Home Work In Your Favour

If home A costs more than home B, then all things being equal it must be because it's more desirable. If you used these strategies so that Australia's financial, business and taxation systems would allow you to buy into a better property, i.e. an "A", then it is reasonable to postulate that it will outperform the "B's" over time and if that comes true, then your capital growth will be higher because (1) your base was higher and (2) you may have positioned yourself for more capital growth by purchasing a more desirable property for the long haul.

Add Value For Less

In case you're starting to think about upgrading your home, you should ask yourself or a licensed real estate agent who is familiar with your area, if your current home could likely benefit from a quick makeover prior to selling it. If so, you can then think of it as ripe in the sense of a "value-add" project. Adopting this mindset requires a shift in thinking to see your own home as an investment asset as much as a lifestyle asset. One major benefit of this is that you do not incur the substantial acquisition costs normally associated with purchasing an investment property (i.e. primarily, stamp duty). Obviously, if you're handy with tools and are happy to do much of the work yourself, then you'll benefit even more from incurring little or no labour costs (it's just a matter of giving up some free time and doing the elbow-work)!

The same applies when looking for a replacement property from which to run your home business as in buying something that could really benefit from some TLC and even better some might say if it's as close to "land value" as possible, you'll be setting yourself up to make some money by enhancing its value through modernisation and other improvements.

Typically, people do the following sorts of things without needing a special license as they would for say plumbing and electrical jobs:

1. Interior and exterior painting
2. Gardening and landscaping
3. Removal and replacement throughout of carpets, door furniture, window treatments and light fittings
4. Installing a new DIY "flat-pack", kitchen bench and cupboards
5. Installing a new bathroom vanity
6. Wall and floor tiling

If this cost you say around $12,000 in materials whilst saving you that much again in labour payments and if it all meant the project might add about $40,000 to the sale price of your home and that it could be completed over say three months by doing it over one day of each weekend. By keeping it simple and not factoring in what else you could've done every Saturday or Sunday to make money (as most people simply wouldn't be doing anything in that respect), then this is a fantastic percentage return of 333% which is more than triple your money over a very brief time frame!

i.e. $40,000 / $12,000 = 3.33r

Be aware that adding value can create further capital gains upon the disposal of that building at a later date but again it should be remembered that these gains can be further deferred in terms of CGT liabilities by reinvesting proceeds into alternative active assets or by other means available within the existing small business discounts and concessions.

Of note, repairs are deductible to the extent of the business use percentage whereas improvements are able to be written off to the same extent at 2.5% per annum for 40 years. Either way, it adds up to more reasons to get busy and do the place up!

Furthermore, if your home business is GST registered, you can then claim GST input tax credits!

Make Your Money When You Buy

For a time, I was employed as a buyer's agent at a prominent Subiaco, WA-based firm. The mission was typically to assist homeowners and investors to make astute purchase decisions and then to execute the deal for them. Inevitably, buyers saved a multiple of the fee they were charged and more importantly, they bought the right property at a good price.

Before, during and since those days, I am continually reminded how the direct property market and in particular the residential market, is very inefficient. Unlike listed companies whose ownership is allotted by shares which investors trade daily and can even value live i.e. in real time, there are everyday examples of mispriced properties being put up for sale for a myriad of reasons.

Accordingly when you rely on the mortgagee valuation (i.e. the lender's valuation), in determining the amount to act as the denominator to be applied against the loan to value ratio (LVR), that will of itself determine the amount of finance provided to you (eg; a $500,000 valuation X 80% LVR = $400,000 maximum loan offer), I recommend you engage a finance broker who will know which lenders will use more than one valuer and of those, which will use the highest valuation provided to them. This is because valuation methods do not comprise an exact science and are still reliant on the individual valuer's own judgment and skill when assessing all factors. Disparity between valuations on the same property at the same time by two or more valuers is not uncommon and it can be significant. Furthermore, the valuer will generally consult the market (properties for sale, properties recently sold and in speaking with local real estate agents) and in so doing, his or her views could be distorted by exceptional or unusual examples of other properties for which the owners have been or are currently asking unreasonable prices or are selling very cheaply but which nevertheless, can cloud the appearance of the true state of a local market. In general, any number of factors can be influential. For example:

1. Motivated seller (whatever their reason/s), sometimes sell at less than market value.

2. Private sellers who are typically motivated by not wanting to pay a sales commission, sometimes fail to conduct proper and sufficient research and underestimate their property's true worth and/or fail to negotiate well.

3. Some selling agents fail to conduct proper and sufficient research only to underestimate the true worth of certain properties and/or also fail to negotiate well.

4. Particularly in a difficult selling market, it is alarming but again not surprising that many selling agents will convince their clients to sell cheaply to effect a quick sale (however without having disclosed the real reason being the agent does not want to work too hard for too long in the pursuit of attaining market price as it makes little difference to the amount of commission they receive). Considering that a say a 2.5% commission on say a $600,000 sale is $15,000 whereas 2.5% on $630,000 is $15,750, it's hardly a massive motivator to some to bust their butt for potentially several months more of home opens etc whereas that $29,250 difference may well cover the stamp duty on the seller's replacement home as well as the conveyance and removalist fees and more so it is very important to the seller! In some cases the difference in selling price to market price can be huge (six figures is not unrealistic and it happens more than you might realise).

5. Furthermore, some agents are reluctant to risk that the property will go "stale" and that the listing will eventually expire only for a new agent to be imminently appointed thereafter. They know that almost without fail, the new agent will convince the seller to immediately drop the price for a quick sale ... ah how the truth can really sting!

The reality is that the woes of the uninformed, lazy, stupid or unconscionably treated seller is however theirs to bear such that consequently, substantial financial advantages can result for you when it is your turn to buy. My advice therefore is to carefully research and expertly negotiate your next property. You may have heard the saying "you make your money when you buy" and this expectation holds true for you if you're willing to put in the time by seeing many properties and to hone your skills otherwise be smart and pay a buyer's agent to do it for you.

Just think of how much easier things could be if you didn't have to generate the additional revenue required to meet those dreaded commercial premises expenses.

21 - Improve Your Lifestyle

Some years ago, a minority of financial planners began to call themselves "lifestyle financial planners" and by this, they purported to mean that their activities would help you to lead a better quality life. I'm not about to put anyone down for that but rather, I simply think that the following information will assist you to understand why I truly believe that the strategies inside this book will serve you better and in ways like nothing else can!

Please consider that in this modern-day world of increasingly congested traffic and difficult and expensive parking, demanding schedules, deadlines a plenty, the difficulty of creating and maintaining positive relationships with management, employees, clients, suppliers and so on, that it's no wonder that stress is the unrelenting common denominator to many illnesses and is indeed a very prominent killer. This leads me to suggest that in having arranged a great many life and income protection insurance applications over the years, that I can categorically state that anybody with a stress-related background always receives extra-special, negative attention from the insurance company underwriters. This is because the insurer's actuaries know full well that the incidence of claims from these sufferers has been, is now and will always be very high. To moderate the risks that could affect the profitability of their portfolios, insurers have to be particularly careful in accepting such applications in the first instance and if they do, they load premiums in a hefty manner, with people commonly paying double or sometimes even more than that of standard-risk applicants.

Generally speaking, for individuals to escape this bleak reality and among other considerations, it's no surprise to me that for some time now, many have been turning to ways in which to back-off from a hectic pace of life and to settle and relax a lot more. A good example of this is franchising. This business model exploded in Australia in the nineties and it was and still is promoted as a way for people to be in business for themselves by following supposedly or hopefully proven guidelines with the support of their franchisor, in order to achieve their desired level of success. It is supposed to take a lot of the stress out of being in business but does it really? Whilst I don't wish to demean the concept or to try and convince anyone of the answer here, I'm simply noting that an abundance of frustrated and/or failed franchisees exist in all parts of the country and across many industries. The critical point is that the franchisee is running their own business and their success is dependent upon a combination of their own business acumen and that of their franchisor's. Alas, there is significant scope for disappointment in that equation because the two must be both congruent and efficient to attain success whereas and sadly, often this is not the case.

Never has it been more apparent than now where we can see how the business ethos is shifting at least in part, from traditional models of yesteryear to the many home-based businesses that are actively flourishing today. This extends across many fields of endeavour ranging from private professional consultation to trades and technical services, to multi-level marketing businesses and more. So for many, a particularly attractive feature of these strategies will be the improvement to current lifestyle that this change will bring and also that this will occur in different ways. Working from home, whilst not everybody's ideal situation, does provide many benefits and these may include among others:

- Wearing comfortable, casual clothing
- Not having to shave or wear makeup every day
- Adopting the most flexible of working hours that can change as it suits you
- The ability to coordinate children's schedule into your own (e.g, pick up from school, work while baby is asleep, etc)
- Keeping your business costs way down by not having separate business premises
- Reducing motoring costs
- Helping the environment by not commuting to work with your car and by not running separate business premises (additional

heating, cooling, lighting, etc)

And more!

The strategies though go much further than this because instead of just changing your workplace to that of home, you can decide to actually change your home as well and when I say change your home, I really mean to upgrade or extend it.

Hence, if in using the proceeds of the sale of a business active asset allowed you to switch from say an average priced home in your town or city or to one that was worth considerably more, immediate lifestyle benefits could result. Let's look at some possible examples of what I'm talking about:

- The ability to send your children to a renowned public school that is outside of your current address' school zone and which also happens to be in a particularly more expensive suburb. Consequently, your children may derive those perceived benefits without you sending them to an expensive private school and this in itself could save you tens of thousands per child throughout their educational years and is money that can also be saved and invested in various ways and perhaps on their behalf or otherwise used at your personal discretion e.g. family holidays, a new car, a boat, investment, etc
- You love early morning surfing and now you can buy that beach side or absolute ocean front home you've always wanted or maybe it's the chic inner CBD high rise condominium with incredible views that seemingly stretch forever or perhaps it's the meandering river views overlooking the yacht club or maybe the hills with their quaint boarded and rammed earth cottages and wooded lots or that rolling green rural acreage you've always yearned for with a few heads of livestock and a couple of horses, etc...hey, it's your dream
- To help your ailing parent/s (e.g. by moving closer to them if they live in an expensive area or by purchasing a larger home perhaps with a "granny flat" to accommodate them)

> ○ Simply to have a more spacious, functional or elegant home, even if in the same suburb or street

How about a very nice and very tax-effective pool, alfresco, dream kitchen or bathroom?

Now whilst these sorts of areas within your home are definitely and will always be inescapably private and domestic in nature and therefore absolutely and of their own accord NOT tax deductible in the slightest, the mother of all riddles perhaps is that regardless, you can absolutely get a tax deduction for a significant part of the interest you incur on borrowings in order to own them (and no I haven't just smoked some weed in case you're wondering)!

It all comes down to what is the property's business use percentage and not how nice or how crappy the place is.

It applies to each of the following:

- ○ Existing properties that are awesome
- ○ hose you want to do up
- ○ Those you want to build from scratch

At first, this might do your head in a little but once you grasp it you'll never think the same way again.

Access to your money after you buy the property

By arranging a line of credit or mortgage redraw facility secured against the property, you can in fact access equity from that property and use it at your absolute discretion (be it for business expansion and/or personal use). Under normal circumstances, most lenders will make available a facility of up to 80% of the equity available (= an 80% "loan to value ratio" or LVR), without insisting you take out and pay for lender's mortgage insurance (LMI), which is an insurance policy designed to protect them and not you. During a credit squeeze however, they may look at imposing LMI at levels from 60% LVR upwards, particularly for borrowers who do not substantiate their earnings at application time (i.e. non-conforming "low doc" or "no doc" loans).

The upside of all this is that the equity in the property is available to the respective owners to do with as they please. E.g. a family living in a house half owned by a company decides with the company to improve the property by adding undercover parking for the use of all the owners as the family has two cars, one owned by the company for exclusive work use (say a ute or van) and one by the family (and minutes of meetings of the company's directors confirm this). The expenses are then incurred by the respective owners in proportion to the "Business Use Percentage" and paid from the two line of credit sub-accounts but in reality, the family (which includes the Company shareholders), has continuous 24 hour access, every day of the year whereas the company Directors do not work the same hours. Of note, fringe benefits tax (FBT), does not apply as the benefit to the "family" is provided by way of their shareholding in the Company and not via anyone's employment by it. Also and again, in this scenario, ownership by the parties would be as Tenants in Common who would each have equal access rights to the entire property and so there is no legal restriction on who can go where etc.

The Company however cannot claim any income tax deductions for any costs associated with the parking area, unless it has been properly segregated and set aside for its exclusive or almost exclusive use. This scenario illustrates the advantage of legally using company funds to improve a property in which the occupants will derive non-business related benefits without the company incurring a FBT liability. From time to time, this could prove very useful as in when the individuals concerned would like to improve the property but are personally cash strapped or otherwise unwilling to borrow the full amount at a time when the company has available funds or borrowing capacity with which to improve its share of the asset (i.e. the business premises).

As you can see, one Tenant in Common (ie; the family/shareholders), is apparently deriving more benefit than the other (the Company) but not in any contrived, unfair or deceitful manner. It's simply just another lifestyle benefit that is inherent to the strategies and yes; many other examples could be expressed but we'll leave it there as it's only a matter of imagination to come up with more.

22 - Age Is No Barrier

Don't let anyone tell you you're too young or too old to live life on your terms and the same goes for when it comes to making your living!

There's only one bottom line depending on which end you're at as either:

1. You're old enough and smart enough to get a home loan meaning you should be old enough and smart enough to run a business or;
2. You're still physically and mentally young enough to run a business in which case, good on you!

Exceptions can apply such as when it's against an employer's policy e.g. you're a bus driver but not allowed to work beyond a particular age or maybe you're a ballet dancer or a professional athlete and there's only so long a life's work available until you're "past your prime".

Otherwise, there's nothing or no-one to force you to stop work at any age so providing you're willing and able, you may derive home business income for the remainder of your natural life.

Frank Genovesi

23 - Retirement Considerations

One of the most important considerations for many people is having sufficient income in retirement to meet their living needs for the rest of their life.

Some people will be well prepared for retirement in benefiting from passive investment income streams (be these within superannuation or otherwise) and for whom any home business income is but a supplement but for many, this won't be the case so having a home business will save those ones from relative poverty in their senior years.

Some people never really retire

It's important to recognise that retirement means different things to different people.

Some may consider the permanent cessation of all work as retirement, whilst others may considerably water that definition down in their own minds and simply "back-off" from work. Just take a good look around and you'll find many people who have been so-called "retired" from their job, career or business and yet they still keep busy doing this or that and not just to keep from being bored but also to make money. Usually they've reached "preservation age" (which means they're old enough to access their super), they're of sound mind and able bodied and with many, many years ahead of them (perhaps half of their life over again thanks to the wonders of medical science coupled with society's overall lower rates of smoking and more moderate drinking etc).

However, let's turn that around for a minute and think about how Australia's ageing population crisis that is set to severely burden future generations of taxpayers and in particular the provision of the age pension. Over the years, various Federal Governments have carved out many enhancements to super and spent big on various publicity campaigns, all aimed at getting people to take very seriously, their personal responsibility to fund their own retirement and as robust as they have been in their endeavour, they have largely failed. The facts are that the great majority of working Australians, who could retire in say the next 20 years or less, are not even close to being on track to financial independence in retirement. This is principally because they have not contributed enough money into superannuation early enough, to allow for the compounding benefits to work sufficiently in their favour. Now they lack both sufficient available time until retirement and copious amounts of spare money to make up for that (obviously, the Federal Government's preferred vehicle in retirement funding policy is still superannuation). This all points to why so many people are working so much longer with the unsurprising reason being that they simply can't afford to retire.

You might already think you're well-prepared for retirement with alternative income streams in place from investments (be these in superannuation or otherwise), so the business income would be but a supplement.

Alternatively, the potential business income may be sufficient on its own to fully support you in retirement.

It's absolutely a question of your needs and your ability to meet those needs from your home business.

Should you sell the property and use the money to fund your retirement?

To answer this, you must assess your current situation, future goals and your options, by asking yourself many questions such as:

- Do I have a positive attitude to life and to business?
- How is my health?
- Are there any hereditary ailments in my family?
- Do I have any personal assets that I can cash in towards retirement?
- Do I already have superannuation?
- If so, how much?
- Do I wish to leave an inheritance?
- Do I wish for my spouse to become a reversionary annuitant (i.e. pick up my pension after I die)?
- Do I have any preferences or aversions to any investments?
- Am I familiar and comfortable with the concept of pooled investments?
- Do I wish to consider setting up my own SMSF?
- Am I looking more for security or growth of capital or a balance?
- Will I need access to large amounts of capital?
- How important is it that I obtain any Centrelink benefits?
- Where will I live?
- What sort of house do I want and how much will it cost?
- What will I do in retirement and will those things be expensive?
- Do I want to help my children or grandchildren?
- What have I given away lately and to whom and what of the potential consequences?
- Do I have any large debts now (e.g; mortgages, loans, tax bills etc)?
- Am I involved in any civil litigation at the moment?
- Am I involved in any disputes or unpleasant dealings that may lead to civil litigation?
- So how much do I really think I'll need every month to live in retirement
- And more!

In arriving at an answer, consider that combinations of the following popular investments can be used to deliver retirement income:

- Federal and State Government Provided Pension Funds
- Industry and Employer Provided Pension Funds
- Fixed-term, Lifetime and Allocated Annuities (via life insurance companies)
- Account Based Pensions (via super funds or retirement savings account providers)
- Investment Properties (directly held)
- Shares (directly held)
- Fixed Interest Products (directly held)

In addition, some people also have part-time businesses or hobby farms etc.

Others may arrange their affairs such that they're entitled to receive part-pensions and/or allowances from Centrelink and even pensions from overseas countries.

All must be considered.

Due to the many questions and answers and the relative weighting that people place on the different matters to be considered, it isn't difficult to imagine that there are also many different possible outcomes to the question of "what is the best thing for me to do about my retirement". The reality is that it can be very challenging to come up with a solution that is "just-the-ticket" in every way. It usually comes down to prioritising and accepting some compromise!

Furthermore, remember that varying degrees of tax effectiveness of retirement income will result depending upon the financial product/s and strategies chosen and in what combinations (and that of course depends upon your "overall" situation) but generally speaking, superannuation which has more recently become a source of tax-free retirement income, will probably continue to be very popular even despite the Turnbull government tweaking that resulted in the 2016 May Federal budget.

Going back to the original question here, let's look then at selling the replacement active asset (i.e. the property) and using say part proceeds to buy a replacement main residence. Let's further assume that your business is run under a company structure and that yours or your spouse or partner and yours, personal share as a tenant in common, is sufficient to be able do that, with the balance (the business' share), being specifically available to fund the retirement of the business owners.

The current contribution eligibility rules to superannuation state that once a member attains age 65, superannuation funds can only accept contributions (subject to the $25,000 p.a. contribution caps announced by ex-Federal Treasurer Morrison, now PM), and only if he or she has worked at least 40 hours in a continuous maximum 30 day period in that same financial year. Also, once a member attains age 75, superannuation funds can no longer accept personal superannuation contributions.

You should also investigate (or ask your financial adviser to on your behalf), whether your superannuation fund has any other restrictions on accepting contributions to the fund.

Hence;

- If the property was sold before you had turned 65 and retired (meaning that you were still allowed to contribute to super), then assuming no unforeseen obstacles, two separate provisions exist within the tax law whereby you can contribute up to $500,000 into superannuation. This means their business would contribute its share of the sale proceeds into a super fund in the name/s of the individual/s (the owner/s) and that it could also enjoy all the gains raised since the acquisition of that property (the subsequent capital gain), as that would be disregarded by the ATO. This in itself is a strategy to harness the long-term growth potential of well-located residential property and to derive untaxed capital gains whilst obtaining income tax deductions throughout the same period.
- If say however you sold the business (including the property) and you were between 65 and 75 years of age and could work

at least 40 hours in a continuous 30 day period in that same financial year, in other words, you met the eligibility rules for super contributions (see above), then "hey presto", you could still make the superannuation contribution.

º In any event, providing the property had been actively used by the business for at least the last 15 years prior to selling it (then in this case of retirement funding purposes as for any other), it would raise no capital gains tax because the "small business 15 year exemption" could be chosen. If, however, throughout the course of utilising the strategy, your business bought and sold various properties, then each particular property would be subject to a new 15 year qualification period to claim this same exemption.

º Finally, "Centrelink" considerations such as receiving at least a part age pension and a senior's card etc., are also very important to many people as it means they can potentially obtain subsidised rates, public transport and other benefits and so it is with great care that this area should be examined to weigh up the potential costs and benefits, with a possible view to ensuring every benefit entitlement to you.

24 - This Suits Many Businesses

Nobody can tell you what business to be in or how many businesses are too many for you as it's your own common sense that needs to prevail on this one.

You're entitled to run a number of home businesses each sharing and/or occupying different spaces in accordance with your circumstances.

Our proprietary Joint Property Sharing Agreement has been put before the ATO many times always to have survived passage.

25 - You Don't Need To Be Wealthy Already

Yep!

Even a first homeowner on a moderate income can do this or perhaps you're recovering from a financially devastating event such as a divorce or business failure!

Don't let your past determine your future!

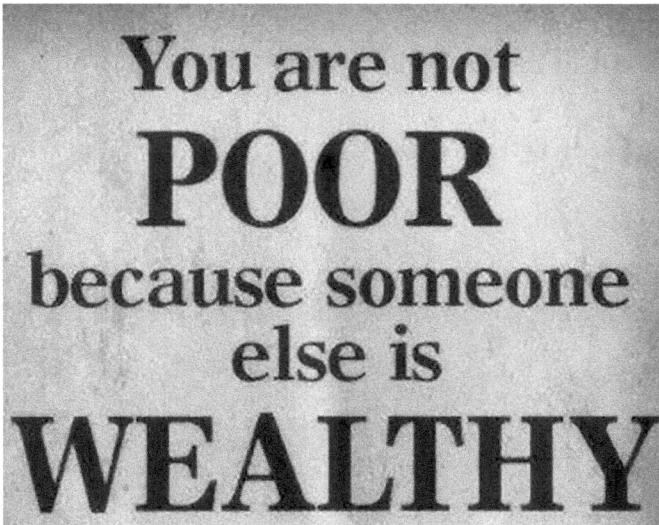
You are not **POOR** because someone else is **WEALTHY**

26 - You Don't Have To Quit Your Job

Why would you do that anyway (unless of course you knew that your home business was going to be sufficiently profitable to warrant it)?

So unless your existing job contract contains a legally enforceable clause to stop you running a home business on the side, then you can spend your free time how you please.

So if you want to really get ahead, get busy!

Frank Genovesi

27 - What's In It for Existing Home Business Owners?

There's a little something I created and that I call the "Twist Exist Re-Structure" (TERS), aptly named being it puts a 'twist' on an "existing" home-based business situation.

The good thing here is that if you already have a home business, then you've already seen the light however this doesn't mean that you're already milking this thing to anywhere near its potential.

Your current home may or may not be a great property for this so the first thing is to determine what's in it for you in terms of where you're already living because if it's not that great, the next thing is to consider extending or upgrading.

As mentioned, in my hundreds of specific interactions when researching all of this, I never met an accountant who knew how to do any of it particularly well let alone anyone that built a practice around it so the odds are that if you use one, you're receiving substandard advice and if you do your own tax work, you're definitely missing out as well. Either way, you're getting screwed blind or you're screwing yourself blind and what's more, you have no idea as to the extent!

I remind you that accountants are overwhelmingly saying that it's not worth claiming the mortgage interest for fear of incurring a massive CGT liability but that's just crazy talk!

Why?

I'm glad you asked!

Even in a low inflation environment where housing prices typically don't tend to rise all that much and even if you lived in Airyfairyland where they were endlessly going up and up, why would you turn your back on big deductions year after year, decade upon decade perhaps, when you know that paying much if any CGT at all is simply a function of poor or no planning coupled with really bad decision making?

My clients certainly don't think that way!

Furthermore, the odds are that you don't know how to correctly zone-off areas within your property to maximise the business use percentage and that's really hurting you. Now on this and possibly with just one simple tweak, you might double, triple or quadruple your deductions because of something akin to knowing where to draw an invisible line on a map.

So what's in it for you guys? Well that just depends on how you look at things and what you do next. Suffice to say though, I have no doubt that for the majority of you, there are thousands if not tens of thousands of dollars every year in unnecessarily paid taxes just going begging.

There's also something very potent in the Income Tax Assessment Act 1936 called "Part IVA" which effectively lets the Commissioner bludgeon you when he can't do so under any other provisions of the many tax laws he administers. It's reserved for cases where he feels you're doing this or that just to get a tax benefit. So unless your personal and business situation contains factors to change the way the ATO might treat you, then the following specific reasons should be enough to stay safe in this regard.

For example:

º   If you're about to stop renting your home business property and to buy one instead, this is a very smart move as you'll obtain low cost home ownership to get you off the treadmill.

º   If you're planning on extending your current home business property because it's getting too small for comfort, the setting aside of the additional resulting area as a Business Use Area will prove very worthwhile from a taxation perspective.

º If you're planning on upgrading your current home business property, the TERS provides a very effective home-business property ownership and control model.

Specifically for companies:

º There are significant long-term financial benefits in combining your personal resources with your private company to own and operate the property (e.g. perhaps no state based land tax to pay due to not meeting the minimum threshold along with other cost savings etc).

º The estate planning advantages are appealing (i.e. the transfer of wealth to dependants and future generations).

º The asset protection advantages appeal as the family home is otherwise and at all times fully exposed to aggressive litigants or;

º There are many retirement planning benefits for the shareholder/s.

Aside from the TERS (ii), irrespective of whether or not you choose a company ownership structure, the TERS provides a legal and ethical transition into a new phase of home-based business ownership that going forward for the long-term, is far more tax-friendly.

On balance and should you prefer to operate as a company, then it's better to make the transition NOW and to thereby incur the associated stamp duty on transfer as it could be some decades that you'll remain in your home and the future savings should far outweigh the current cost of the transition.

If however you want to remain a sole trader or in a partnership, you should still start claiming those occupancy expenses now as when you may eventually sell, you'll still be able to navigate the waters to a very low or no CGT position so there's heaps to gain and nothing to lose in that.

At last you can enjoy the peace of mind of a potential totally CGT free outcome, depending on how you apply the rules in future that is, if and when you ever sell your home due to downsizing in retirement or perhaps for some other reason.

28 - But I've Paid Off My Mortgage

Well then, at first glance I suppose you'd be forgiven in thinking that none of this fancy stuff is going to work for you but let me just say that would be hasty.

Remember this is mostly about attitude hence if you want the benefits, you must change your thinking.

A simple example is where you sell your current home that you've paid off and which is worth say $500,000 and buy an upgraded one for say $750,000 to suddenly again have a mortgage (this time around it's for $250,000 and let's forget about transaction costs just for now).

The difference between this and the last time you bought a home was you did your fancy-special homework first and chose a property that provides you with say a 33% Business Use Percentage (or whatever). If it suits you, a company structure might be selected being the company (not you), is liable for the loan repayments including the fully tax deductible interest.

Effectively then, you get to upgrade your home using a significant portion of pre-tax money to pay towards your fully deductible business loan of your premises (that just happens to be situated at your new home).

Of course if you prefer, you can also do this without a company in place but the numbers and rules will be a little different.

It's worth careful thought don't you think?

29 - But My Business Already Runs From Commercial Premises?

I again refer you to Chapter 9, Lowers The Cost Of Home Ownership At Any Purchase Price.

At any given time in any given property market, you must consider the impact of breaking a lease or selling your commercial property. Additionally you must consider any likely loss of passing trade from a busy street or shopping mall etc. While all this talk about quitting your commercial premises might be a good idea, for whatever reason however, unfortunately the timing may not be right so do bear this in mind.

Notwithstanding the above, there are still good reasons to contemplate it all. By thinking outside the box, you can perhaps use your existing knowledge to create an "offshoot" business which would home based. This is important to grasp because under the tax law, you can't bring work home from your job to claim a deduction for the work space set aside for that purpose as the courts have ruled as that such arrangements are carried out purely as a matter of convenience.

Accordingly therefore, the trick is to do something at home that is different to that as done at your commercial premises and providing it is done under a separate ABN and has a fair amount of commercial sense attached, it is then reasonably arguable before the tax office that it is a different business despite implementation of knowledge etc as garnered from the existing business.

Example 1: You own and operate a restaurant but also have some special recipes. Accordingly you write a cookbook and sell it on a special purpose website that has nothing to do with the restaurant or maybe you create packaged frozen meals for distribution to supermarkets.

Example 2: You're a mechanic who found a reliable part that you can import say from China and sell to other mechanics at a profit of course, still whilst saving them money.

These are potentially separate businesses that can make for themselves a "place of business" within your home and from which, sizeable business deductions may arise.

I'll leave it up to you to imagine your own possibilities.

30 - A Big Fat Tax-Free Windfall Anyone?

It may be possible to arrange your business and financial affairs such that you create some tax deductible business debt where none otherwise exists.

If you've already paid off your mortgage, then there's no loan interest to claim and therefore not much reason to do any of this ... right?

Hmm, maybe not!

You could start a business under a company structure and that company buys a "share" of your home at fair market value and let's say it's for six figures. Now with a fully tax deductible loan on business premises, the company enjoys significant deductions for the interest on the loan that it took to pay you out.

And it just gets better because as the owner of the company, you pocket the purchase price (tax free), that the company just paid to acquire its financial interest on the title and presuming you haven't been using your home to produce income, the dosh is protected by the main residence cgt exemption.

You can now spend, save or invest that money however you wish!

Happy days!

31 - Sure Beats Super

When I say super, I mean all of industry, state and Commonwealth Government, public offer & self-managed superannuation funds!

Total negation of tax on contributions, earnings and exit

The good news is my strategies allow you to manage your affairs at any point in time and/or over the course of time such that very little if any capital gains tax needs to be paid in the event you sell your home business property for a tidy sum (fingers crossed in that department for when the time comes)!

Alternatively and if for example you contribute the capital proceeds of a business sale into a super fund on behalf of one or more of the owners, then despite even claiming the small business retirement exemption (meaning no capital gains tax would be paid on the otherwise CGT assessable component of the business sale or on its particular active assets that were sold), some significant disadvantages would still remain. In saying therefore, please consider the following:

I. **No contributions tax:** To obtain a tax deduction on either of self-employed, employee salary sacrificed or employer SGC contributions, one must accept that a flat 15% Federal tax applies on all such contributions and that this significantly reduces the amount of money working for you such that long term wealth accumulation is greatly reduced due to the lost compounded benefits over the years. Imagine the horror if your super fund or financial adviser charged you a 15% fee on every contribution! By contrast, my strategies provide significant tax advantaged retirement benefits with no tax levied on the purchase price or any subsequent loan repayments in regard to the replacement active asset (i.e. the replacement property). In fact, even local and state property taxes are reduced by virtue of the income tax system via the process of business tax deductions.

II. **No earnings tax:** For all super funds that derive income in any given tax year, a tax is automatically levied upon it at up to 15% p.a. This becomes payable once the Trustee of the fund has lodged its annual tax return and that return has been assessed. Conversely, with my strategies you pay none nor any equivalent disguised under another name. You will recall that property, even if partially owned by one or more individuals but used as their primary residence, still enjoys untaxed capital growth on that component due to the CGT main residence exemption.

Furthermore, there is no investment income (i.e. rent), generated by this personal ownership component thus neither is any income tax raised on a year-to-year basis.

As for the business ownership component, because the asset is active and not passive, again there is also no income (i.e. rent) and hence again, no year-to-year income tax issues arise as a consequence. For the business' part, all future growth in capital value of the property remains exempt from assessment for capital gains tax purposes, providing the property is actively used in the business on an ongoing basis. This may induce some people to never fully retire and to work a minimum amount (whatever that might be from time to time), to satisfy any future ATO determination of what it means to carry on a business. Of course if you were to decide to fully retire, you could under such circumstances, sell the property and contribute any otherwise assessable amount for capital gains, into a super fund (but only whilst you were still in accumulation phase). Accumulation phase simply means you haven't yet fully retired and you're still contributing or able to contribute to super and under certain circumstances, this can be up to age 70. The amount left over from your personal share of the property may itself be sufficient to purchase another home but of course that would depend on your needs and aspirations in retirement, which is a very personal matter and is one that does warrant careful consideration. Not forgetting also, that if you've retired and had owned and used the property for the last 15 years or more as an active asset, that the proceeds of sale would be CGT free in any event, and that contributing to super would not be a consideration for purposes of reducing or minimising CGT.

III.   **No exit tax:** When accessing super in retirement, you must ascertain whether the fund contributed to was taxed or untaxed. Hence in relation to any post June 1983 component of an eligible termination payment (ETP), from those funds that have already been taxed, as from 01 July 2007, the great news is that no tax is payable on pensions or lump sums drawn. Further great news is that Reasonable Benefit Limits (RBL's) have been long abolished. However, for untaxed funds, a 15% tax applies to the first tier with 30% on any amounts over that. Please note that the Medicare levy must be added to the above tax rates except where the nil rate applies.

Danger of exceeding lifetime retirement exemption of $500,000

The small business retirement exemption has an inherent condition prohibiting you from claiming any more than $500,000 in your lifetime from it and very disturbingly, this is NOT indexed. As many businesses already have net assets of between $500,000 and $6million, they will find this dreadful so instead, they may wish to consider the strategies as detailed herein on the basis that among other things, they pass the $6million net asset value test.

Total investor and user control

With institutionally managed super funds, it is the fund manager and not you whose job it is to make the day to day decisions about which assets to invest in or to sell-down or sell-off altogether. From time to time, they may get it right or wrong and either way, you cannot interfere in that process. Considerably more flexible however, is the self-managed superfund (SMSF), where the appointed trustee can do all of those things but the Superannuation Industry Supervision Act's legislation (SIS) which covers all super funds, prohibits beneficiaries of the funds deriving any personal use benefit of the assets contained in the funds. E.g. you cannot buy a house to put it in your SMSF and then use it as your primary residence or even buy art or furniture etc as a SMSF investment and then use these in your home.

When it comes to business real property, the general rule is that 100% of its use must be for business purposes. Furthermore and generally speaking, to derive a benefit from any superfund, you have to be at least 55 years of age and retired. Furthermore, you should consider that the decision-making and ultimate responsibility for the management of the SMSF rests with the Trustee(s) who is/are normally a member(s) of the Fund or an incorporated company controlled by members of the Fund. These responsibilities include all relevant administrative and compliance tasks that are normally performed for a fee with public offer or industry funds. In order to satisfy these responsibilities, a trustee must remain familiar with the current legislation, rules and regulations affecting the operation of SMSF's. This is a huge task for the average person who is neither trained nor skilled in these matters. While I and other competent advisers in this area are available for a fee, the operation of the Fund ultimately remains the responsibility of the trustee. Particular breaches of such obligations are considered very serious and strict punishments can apply. Again, my strategies circumvent all of these issues because within the ambit of the law, you can live and work in the property rather as you please and modify your routine to suit yourself on a day to day basis.

Access to your money

Unless you meet specific conditions of release such as permanent departure from Australia or financial hardship, once your money is contributed to superannuation, it's absolutely locked-in for what can be a very a long time. The permitted access age is called your preservation age and it is reached when you are somewhere between 55 and 60 (depending on whether you were born before 1960 or somewhere in between then and the end of 1965) and then again, only if you've retired. So and particularly if your preservation age is still a fair way off and where meantime your outlook or circumstances change such that you feel you should've done things differently, unfortunately by having opted for heavy regular and/or lump sum super contributions instead of a home business strategy, then as a result of such stringent conditions imposed on accessing your superannuation, you'd better be prepared to take a deep breath and accept that what is done is done.

In this regard, the saving grace of the strategies is that you can borrow against the equity in the property (typically using a line of credit or a redraw facility) and which can be done at any time and practically free of interference by anyone except the lender (i.e. mainly only if you default).

On the other hand, if you don't want to do that, you can sell your home business property and do any number of things such as:

1. Replace it again with another property and continue along your merry way
2. Replace it with a totally different type of active business asset (maybe just buy another business or whatever) and say goodbye to the strategies
3. Pay whatever tax you must, say goodbye to the strategies and then do whatever you like
4. As in (3) above, but pop some into super anyway as this can minimise any tax that might otherwise be payable in concert with boosting your retirement outlook

And;

No Conditions of Release with SBRB

Further to the above on preservation age, there are other conditions of release which are

º   you reach age 65
º   you reach preservation age and permanently retire

- you die
- you are permanently incapacitated
- your employment is terminated and the benefit is less than $200, or
- you are a lost member who is found and the benefit is less than $200.

Also available are:

- Compassionate grounds
- Provisions for the terminally ill and;
- The "Transition to Retirement" rules.

No management fees

Buying a home business property is nothing like institutionally managed super funds because there are no ongoing asset management fees or annual member fees and this can result in a huge positive difference to your end retirement benefit over many years or in some case decades. Further to this, there are also no ongoing financial adviser's "funds under advice" fees to reduce your final payout.

As for SMSF's, the costs of operating one depends on the types of investments held, the type of administration or trustee services used and the size of the fund. Managing and investing in a SMSF can be more expensive than with a public offer fund. I just like many other accountants and/or financial advisors can advise on the likely range of costs and viability of doing so.

However, an honest assessment would surely signal that there are no reasons to get someone to manage your home business property (i.e. your asset), given you're living in it and nor should you need ongoing advice with it. So it should be concluded that not paying those fees is normal under a home business strategy and not some form of misguided and false savings due to not having retained appropriate management and advice.

No annual audit fees

SMSF's must be audited each year and that does cost money. How much depends of course on the complexity of the trust deed and again upon the number and types of investments held by the fund. To suggest $400 a year for a typical fund would not be uncommon though and there again, depending on how many years out from retirement you are, that could be a lot of money (not counting the normal inflationary trend of professional fees charged by auditors).

A self managed super fund (SMSF), may only borrow in certain limited circumstances

In September 2007, S.67(4A) was inserted into the 1993 Superannuation Industry (Supervision) Act (Cth), allowing such funds to borrow to invest. So if you're the Trustee of your own SMSF and you really want to go down this path, then be prepared for some rigorous compliance and serious financial and personal commitment due to matters such as:

º Expecting to pay significant fees to set it all up including having a limited recourse borrowing arrangement so the trustee of your fund can buy an asset for the fund or in other words, unless you're made of money, don't just jump in blindly, simply because you're now allowed to

º Expecting to shell out good money for good advice from an accountant and/or financial adviser because you'll probably need it being as the rules are complex and especially to compensate or protect the lender for the nature of the limited recourse, the lender may:

   º Require you to obtain independent financial and/or legal and/or taxation advice at your expense
   º Charge a higher interest rate on the borrowing
   º Insist on a lower LVR; or
   º Request a personal guarantee from the members of the fund.

(Note): Some of these requests by the lender **may** cause the arrangement to fall foul of the investment laws in the SIS Act and Regulations.

1. Expecting that in the event of an audit under the SIS Act, you'll be required to evidence that all assets bought in this manner are consistent with the fund's investment objective and strategy.
2. Expecting to "cop it on the chin" and to probably keep on working for many years or to retire a lot poorer if you're nearing what you thought was to be your retirement but have borrowed heavily for a property that has fallen significantly in value and you don't have the luxury of time to wait for capital values to recover ... i.e. can you really see yourself starting all over again at that late age?

Please also consider that member/s of SMSF's may generally not receive any personal benefits from the fund until after they have reached their preservation age and so this completely rules out buying a property to live in until then = not much fun!

Finally and in complete contrast to superannuation, as previously explained, my strategies allow you to borrow against the property and for whatever purpose you wish without all of these "rules" hanging over you!

32 - How Does Some Nice, Tax-Subsidised Travel Sound?

If all you have is just a job, then ordinary commuting is not a tax deductible expense whereas all trips from your home business property e.g. to see clients, grab supplies or to generally run around on business matters, are deductible in accordance with the general rules on business vehicles and this alone could save you thousands of dollars every year in tax!

Of course, every business owner is entitled to claim legitimate travel costs as well so if your business can justify the expense to send you across the country or indeed even the globe, then while you're away doing whatever, you need to eat and sleep right? Whether or not you travel business class, stay in really nice hotels and eat in good restaurants is up to you and only you and regardless of which, your expenses are deductible (subject to ATO limits set on a country-by-country basis).

The fact that maybe whilst in London, Paris or wherever, you hit the town at night to catch great shows and concerts etc, doesn't alter the trip's legitimacy hence your main expenses are still good to claim (but not the show and concert tickets), ok?

33 - Wanna Help Save The Planet?

Further to my thoughts on saving money and tax by not commuting, that also means you're reducing your own carbon footprint by limiting your vehicle emissions.

The same applies to running appliances as by giving up your business premises for a home office, there's only one fridge, air conditioner, heater, coffee machine, alarm system, stereo and so on running.

Make no mistake friend, that some weird looking frog, insect or furry little critter somewhere will thank and maybe even love you for it so there are your warm and fuzzies!

34 - Certain Furnishings Equate To Business Plant & Equipment On The Balance Sheet

So you've seen an awesome desk for your home office but it's expensive.

Aw what the heck!

It's plant and equipment remember so that means under Division 40 ITAA 1997, it can be immediately written-off for tax purposes (within applicable limits) or alternatively written down over the remainder of its useful life. At time of writing, there's almost a year to go under the $20,000 instant asset write-off so that's gotta be good - right?

This thinking applies to the grandfather clock, the sofa, the rug, the artwork, the cabinet, the workbench, tools etc, etc.

Basically, all "business stuff" found in and about in your office, waiting room, reception area, back office, studio, workshop and so on are business assets that form part of your business balance sheet.

To the extent these are used by the business in deriving assessable income, any interest on loans taken out to buy these are also deductible expenses to rest on on the profit and loss statement.

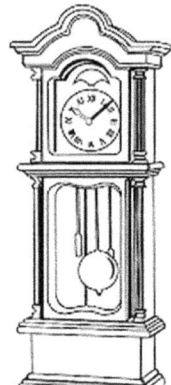

35 - Explore Potential Ventures

I appreciate that it's possible you may be thinking ... "sure this sounds great and all but just what home business can I or should I run"?

It's most probably in your own interest to start thinking about this aspect of your life sooner rather than later as every day you wait is surely costing you money in which case, further down are some possibilities to contemplate.

If you see something you like and want to run with it great, although firstly be sure to do some business planning, cash flow projections and profit forecasts to help ensure you don't go down a path of disappointment and ask me or someone savvy for help if you feel the need.

However if nothing here appears to your liking, don't despair and perhaps keep looking here, there and everywhere and do keep your thinking cap on as by having these thoughts uppermost in your mind, you will eventually create your own destiny.

Perhaps you could investigate any one or more of the following as legitimate avenues to a home based business:

- Trading in financial instruments such as; shares, cfd's
- Foreign exchange,
- Precious metals
- Antiques
- Vintage guitars, cars and jewellery
- Modern jewellery
- Art and other exotics and collectables
- Property development (alone or in syndication)
- Property renovation & resale
- A bed and breakfast
- An Uber taxi

- A micro agribusiness of your own
- Animal husbandry (horses, alpacas etc)
- A repair business for appliances, computers, musical instruments etc
- Piano tuning
- Dressmaking and alterations
- Handyman and/or gardening services
- A qualified trade (electrician, plumber, carpenter, etc)
- Converting any passion or pastime into a commercial venture (art, sport, music, song writing, music production, fiction writing, modelling, fishing, camping, food, wine, martial arts, physical & personal training, movies, travel … basically – you name it)
- Writing a book or an e-book on something you're knowledgeable about for hopeful publication or self publication in physical and online stores and/or from your own website
- Hiring a "ghost-writer" and selling the work as your own (don't worry, it's perfectly legal)
- Blogging for money
- Acquiring or making "stuff" for sale at the markets or online on sites such as "Gumtree" and/or your own website
- An eBay store selling just about anything
- Tuition in singing, playing a musical instrument, languages, computers, primary or high school maths, English, science, etc
- Business coaching
- Mortgage broking
- Professional services (aAccounting, architecture, engineering, law, medicine, dentistry, physio, chiro, podiatry, etc)
- Legal services
- Financial planning
- Real estate agency
- Architecture
- Building
- Personal development
- Life coaching
- Spirituality
- Public speaking
- Web design
- Website SEO

- ⚬ Translation services
- ⚬ Proof-reading
- ⚬ Dog grooming/washing/training
- ⚬ Article writing
- ⚬ Conveyancing
- ⚬ Bookkeeping
- ⚬ Virtual assistant
- ⚬ Online affiliate marketing i.e. where you set up a website and to promote other people's goods and services for commission
- ⚬ Direct selling (Amway, Nutrimetics, Ursana, Bessemer, Avon, Enjo, Herbalife, Mary Kay, Nuskin, Tupperware, Lingerie Party Plans, Linen Party Plans etc)

And so on and so forth.

The key is to use your imagination and you'll surely find something that can be both enjoyable and profitable!

Additionally, why not search online under something like "home based business opportunities Australia" and take it from there.

Remember to keep it real and ...

Good hunting!

Frank Genovesi

36 - No Restrictions on Future Business Activities

Regardless of business structure, you can run as many businesses as you like and across as many industries and professions as you can handle.

You can also chop and change as you wish.

Just be commercially sensible about it!

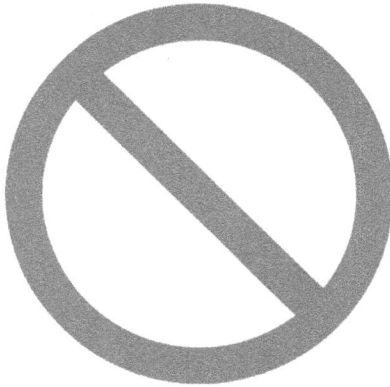

37 - General Insurance

There's no sense in going down this track to create this great new thing only and without any warning, to have the rug pulled out from under you.

Imagine the horror of your fabulous home business property burning to the ground only to find your insurer refuses to pay and that they are legally entitled to adopt that position.

Alternatively a customer is injured at your home and proves it's your fault and your plain old home insurance policy doesn't cover you for a home business.

Accordingly it's vital that you disclose your home business to your insurer so it can reassess the risk and offer you either standard or revised terms.

Even if you are turned down flat at least you'll know where you stand.

Most domestic house and contents policies will only offer very limited cover and so you're best course is to seek out an insurer who is actively looking for home business customers as it will offer more comprehensive and better cover.

If in doubt, consult a general insurance broker.

38 - Asset Protection

Firstly for the bad news:

1. In running your home business as a sole trader or in a partnership, your home is always fully exposed to aggressive litigants.
2. In addition and as a layman, my understanding of legal precedent is that if you have a shareholding in a private company, you can expect a court as and when appropriate, to "look through" the ownership structure and to include the value of that shareholding in your pool of personal assets without regard to the legal status of the company as a separate entity. Hence, if you alone own your company or alternatively if say all of the two or more shareholders are being individually sued on a non-company related matter or matters, then as you should expect, there is no asset protection in any of this.

Now for some better news however, being that we cannot lose what is not ours!

Accordingly if a business property is owned as tenants in common between two or more individuals along with a company or trust, this can therefore in certain cases, diminish risks in litigation being a company or trust business ownership structure protects the business' holding of the property to whatever extent the home is not in the personal name of whoever is being sued.

No doubt the courts will look at the financial interest attributed to each tenant in common as expressed on the Certificate of Title then next, to the shareholding of any individual of the company's portion.

Whilst each case will no doubt turn on the surrounding facts and circumstances, the benefit here is a lesser degree of likelihood of an individual shareholder of a company being sued if that person has insufficient assets worth targeting i.e. in a commercially pragmatic context.

Another benefit is that even if an action proceeds to trial, this ownership structure can cushion the effect of a loss in court being there would be fewer assets at risk.

E.g. if a shareholder's non-director/non-shareholding spouse or de-facto partner were to be sued on what is a non-company related matter such as drink driving causing bodily harm, the strategy protects the business' financial interest in the property because the person being sued has no right to the assets of The company and so the courts cannot include such in that person's pool of assets if it were considering damages.

Another aspect to consider is that all parties might hold their interests as tenants in common. E.g. with say a husband and wife or perhaps two siblings, the property would be divided into two personal parcels of ownership and a third for the company. So per the previous paragraph, if the person being sued is ordered by a court to pay up, then only their personal share is exposed. If say there were three siblings as shareholders and one was being sued over something non-company related, then the other two individuals' portions as well as two-thirds of the company portion, would be immune to a legal action.

Conversely if one was to be sued over a business matter, adopting the strategy wouldn't help in terms of asset protection as the assets of the business could be targeted in any event but at least there is no downside.

I admit this is not the most effective asset protection strategy available but it definitely does provide some benefit in certain situations. Hence, to exclude a home business strategy from your plans just because the asset protection is not completely bullet-proof, is I think, a big call to make given the vast array of benefits it has to offer. Again and to confirm any doubts you may have in relation hereto, please check with a good lawyer and be sure to balance all the points I've raised.

39 - Cashflows And Costings

Here's a really simple tabular worksheet for you to complete, otherwise for your accountant or financial adviser and be sure to include GST where applicable.

Disposal of Existing Residence	Acquisition of a New Residence/Business Premises or an Interest by your Company in Your Existing Home	Other (as applicable to you & including GST)
$_____ Real estate agent's fee $_____ Mortgage security discharge fee $_____ Other $_____ Other $_____ Other	$_____ Buyers agent's fee $_____ Stamp Duty on purchase (where applicable) $_____ Mortgage stamp duty $_____ Mortgage registration fee $_____ Pest inspection $_____ Building inspection $_____ Building Insurance $_____ Other $_____ Other $_____ Other	$_____ Moving costs $_____ Loan application fee $_____ Financial planner's fee $_____ Accountant's fee $_____ Business Broker's fee $_____ Valuation of business assets $_____ Solicitor's fee for advice for potentially up to three properties (i.e. sell home and business premises to buy a replacement home business property) $_____ Other

TOTAL UP FRONT COSTS: $_____

Frank Genovesi

40 - Advanced Cash Flow Applications

Consolidate Your Personal Debts (For Sole Traders and Partnerships)

Given that the money your business outlays in earning its assessable income is generally deductible (unless it's for a private, domestic or capital purpose), there's good reason to consolidate your non-tax deductible personal debts such as car loans, store cards, credit cards and personal loans etc, directly into your home loan. Consider that if your $350,000 home loan which was say 50% deductible by way of running a home business, was suddenly increased by refinancing into it, any or all of the example other debts just mentioned above, then it is conceivable that it might rise to say $400,000 thereby meaning an extra $25,000 of deductible debt is now attributed to the business.

Variation of Income Tax Instalments - Yet Another Level

If you run a business as a sole trader or in partnership, you might find yourself running at a loss (particularly in the early stages of development). If so and providing you also happen to have a regular job, you can ask your employer to vary (i.e. reduce) your Pay As You Go tax withheld amounts each pay period to account for the reduced annual income you are anticipating.

To do this with reasonable accuracy, you'd need to forecast what the loss would be for the remainder of the tax year and go from there to establish the new, lower, taxable income for your employer to base the lower withholding tax amount.

As you may know, people sometimes do this when losing money on shares, managed funds and investment properties (that sort of loss is commonly known as negative gearing and in this new context, you'd be negative gearing your own home).

The point in telling you this is that you can use the extra regular money in your pay packet to cushion the blow as you grow your new home business rather than wait until you've submitted your tax return in order to get your refund.

If you overestimate the loss you will be expected to pay back any excessive amount of PAYG tax withheld so a conservative approach is best adopted.

There's no right or wrong on whether or not to do this as it's simply a choice you have albeit the ATO must approve the application to vary the instalments.

Capitalising Interest On The Business Loan - This Is Seriously Powerful Stuff

If you have a large enough buffer in your business loan facility, then why not stop paying interest, instead to let it compound upon itself thus incurring your business more interest over and over?

A crazy idea?

Maybe not. This frees up all your otherwise committed business loan interest repayments allowing you to instead make additional payments to your non-deductible home loan (that's right — to pay down the "bad debt" even faster and more cheaply).

To avoid drama with the tax office however, you need to consider two aspects:

1. In terms of claiming deductions that the ATO may argue are "non-deductible" for business purposes, we suggest you only claim the original interest and not any capitalised "interest-on-interest" so be sure to keep good records and;
2. If you intend to operate your home business under a private company structure, then you need to bear in mind the rules at Division 7A, of Part 111 of ITAA 1936 as surrounding the making of loans to shareholders.

Amongst other things, you would also need a complying "Division 7A Loan Agreement" and to keep the loan from being deemed a dividend, you'd need to ensure the yearly payments are made by June 30th. I therefore strongly suggest you firstly take personal advice before you "try this at home" but don't worry too much as it isn't as scary or as hard as it sounds.

Why Not Convert Your Job Into A Business?

If you have a job that you could largely do from home, there's nothing to stop you asking your employer to "let you go" as an employee and to hire you as a "contractor" instead?

This entails making a satisfactory and practical arrangement to swap your job for doing that work from home in your own business (and where necessary this may require you e.g. to still pop into the office etc. once or twice a week for a client or "staff" meeting etc), otherwise, however, you definitely work at home but now provide your ex-employer with "Tax Invoices" that show your Australian Business Number (ABN), for the work you do.

This is an advanced cash flow strategy because small businesses can pay tax at the end of the year meaning that you have access to those funds meantime to reduce debt and therefore loan interest and/or to reinvest into the business as working capital in the hope of it helping to produce additional profit whereas as an employee, tax is deducted from your regular pay meaning you can only avail yourself of your lower net pay to do whatever with.

E.g. If you previously earned $100,000 p.a in a job whereas you now have a contract for that same amount of work per annum, you simply invoice the $100,000 out (perhaps fortnightly or monthly), to your ex-employer who is now your "client". Next, depending on the percentage of business use area you set aside at home coupled with the size of the mortgage, this might raise anywhere from say $10,000 to $100,000 p.a in deductions (or perhaps even more as depending on your circumstances). Regardless of the amount, you can then offset your newly established property deductions against your newly established business income effectively allowing you to earn that same $100,000 completely tax-free. Is this too good to be true? No; however, it does require careful planning and the right circumstances.

Before doing this, there are some downsides that must be considered such as:

1. You'd forfeit your right to future employer superannuation support plus other entitlements such as sick leave, holiday pay, public holidays and long service leave and so you'd need to weigh it all up to make an informed and properly considered choice and further when negotiating the contract price for your services.
2. In addition, you'd have to carefully watch the "80% rule" under the Personal Services Income rules which means that if you find yourself needing to rely on passing this test, that you must ensure that less than 80% of your future business income comes from your past employer. To play it safe in this regard, just find some new clients to the tune of 20% or more of your annual turnover!

In so doing, you need to further ensure the arrangement is genuine and not contrived as to be considered a contractor, you'll need to tick a number boxes

I.e: **Ability to subcontract/delegate:** You're free to subcontract/delegate the work meaning you can pay someone else to do the work.

Basis of payment: You're paid for a result achieved based on the quote you provided.

Equipment, tools and other assets: You provide all or most of the equipment, tools and other assets required to complete the work and you don't receive an allowance or reimbursement for the cost of this equipment, tools and other assets.

Commercial risks: You assume the commercial risks and are legally responsible for your work as well as liable for the cost of rectifying any defect in your work.

Control over the work: You have freedom in the way the work is done, subject to the specific terms of any contract or agreement.

Independence: You are operating your own business independently of your ex-bosses and you perform services as specified in your contract or agreement and are free to accept or refuse additional work.

On the surface then, it would seem that under the right circumstances and if you can raise some substantial property based deductions that the balance could be clearly in your favour to adopt this advanced mechanism (which is way beyond ordinary cash-flow strategies). Furthermore and beyond tax, there are an array of lifestyle benefits on offer when you are your own boss and arguably none moreso than when you work at or from home.

Conclusion

In recapping the opportunities provided in running with a super smart home business strategy, here are ten key questions to help get yourself safely over the line.

1. If you have a significant active business asset or assets that you could sell and to then use the money to re-invent your personal and business life by potentially living in a fabulous home in a great area, coupled with other things we've figured out, all of which provides you with a host of amazing advantages, wouldn't you look at it closely? ... Enter the "SBRB"!

2. If you're already working from home, why wouldn't you want every benefit legally possible? ... Enter the "TERS"!

3. If you're employed publicly or privately as say a teacher, a secretary, a welder, a brickie, a Doctor, a nurse, an accountant or a chef (obviously we could just go on and on) and you had a good business idea that you could put into motion in your spare time without quitting your current employment and that one day might even replace your current income (but of course if you want to dive in full-time from the start then that's entirely up to you); wouldn't the prospect of earning that new main income or extra income together with a long list of other benefits be very tantalising? ... Enter the "HBRS"!

4. What if for example you're a contractor or a subbie (trade or professional - it doesn't matter); now you can base yourself from home in a way like never before but the difference is you're going to be pampered with advantages you've been lead to believe were impossible ... Enter the "HBRS"!

5. So you've got a hobby, you play sport, you're in a band, you love to paint or have some other passion - yee-ha! Jump on buddy 'cause if you can commercialise that (and it's never that hard if you think outside the square), then this just might make your day and secure your future ... Enter the "HBRS"!

6. So you're an internet and/or eBay addict huh? As long as you're into selling stuff and not always buying, this could be perfect for you! ... Enter the "HBRS"!

7. If you're into collecting say art or antiques, share trading or even building a substantial property investment portfolio, then consider instead running these investor activities as a bona-fide business (at least to some extent), in order to reap a pile of benefits over and above those mere financial ones you are already trying to attain? ... Enter the "HBRS"!

8. If you're already in business and perhaps leasing a studio, shop, workshop or office and reckon that you could still make a good living doing it in a more relaxed and flexible manner from home instead, wouldn't you want to find out the smartest and most financially beneficial way of rearranging your affairs to make that happen? ... Enter the "SBLB"!

9. If you just can't afford a property of your own to live in and/or work from, wouldn't you be glad to have a Procedure available that lets you approach someone close to you (e.g; parent, sibling, friend), to be a co-owner of your newly proposed business premises and even the business itself if that's what everyone wants and which will be situated within your new home and best off, that everyone will benefit? ... Enter the "COWB"!

10. If you love someone enough that you really want to help them get ahead and in such a way that you can benefit financially also, then how about helping them to buy a good property in a good area to live in and from which they'll also run a home-based business (and maybe you can even run it together if you like), and with a tonne of benefits? ... Enter the "COWB"!

In having carefully read to this end point, you're undoubtedly one very smart, tenacious and switched-on cookie. Now if only you're willing to NOT settle for having read this book but to actually implement one of the strategies, then you not only deserve success but you're highly likely to find it simply because you're HUNTING for it (and that's the sole point of this book i.e. to give something valuable to those who are looking to make for themselves a better life) and who are NOT willing to let that responsibility fall solely to others like financial planners, accountants and fund managers, etc.

In closing, I can't emphasise enough that if you've been nodding your head to much of what you've learned here, then NOW is the time to start conjuring up some sensible commercial and lifestyle plans (NOT TOMORROW) and that you really MUST get in touch quickly (i.e. to strike while the iron is hot), otherwise you're at grave risk of wilting before some uninformed "do-gooder be they a friend, family member or a professional adviser (and whom however now knows a lot less than you), successfully talks you out of it. Worse still, they won't have your open mind and sufficient common sense to have read this book before forming their opinion.

On the other hand if you do happen to find someone intelligent whom you respect, who reads this book and still thinks it's too good to be true, ask them to contact me and I'll happily answer their questions.

The future is coming so whatever it takes, make your way with a spring in your step.

It's all there to be done.

The best of planning to you!

Contact Details

Frank Genovesi

Managing Director
Genovesi Enterprises Pty Ltd
ABN: 93 074 529 589
T/As; Intellisolve:

Website: www.intellisolve.com.au
LinkedIn: https://au.linkedin.com/in/frankgenovesi
Email: frank@intellisolve.com.au
Skype: genovesi111

Adviser training and licensing enquiries welcome!

Frank Genovesi

www.ingramcontent.com/pod-product-compliance
Lightning Source LLC
Chambersburg PA
CBHW050102210326
41519CB00015BA/3794